AF504120

'LLEYN PENINSULA BY CAR'

This guide book contains exact but simple directions for the motorist who wishes to explore the Lleyn Peninsula and the western fringe of Snowdonia, starting from a convenient base such as Porthmadog or Caernarfon, or any resort in the Lleyn itself. The Lleyn has a long and varied coastline; nearly all the main resorts are in the south, where there are many magnificent beaches, but from Abersoch to the western tip of the peninsula — the 'Land's End' of Wales — the coast becomes increasingly rugged, and this feature dominates the north-western coast as far as Morfa Nefyn; even so the cliffs and rocks are broken by a number of sandy beaches and coves. Much of the coast, however, is half a mile or more from the nearest road, and footpaths are few and rarely marked.

As you drive north-eastwards from Nefyn towards Caernarfon there is a miniature mountain range, dominated by the triple peaks of Yr Eifl — 'The Rivals' — the highest only 564 metres (1850 ft), but impressive because they are close to the sea and backed by low ground to the south. To the east of our routes lie the great mountains of Snowdonia and diversions described in the text take you into beautiful mountain valleys, and within sight of Snowdon itself. This guide can be used in conjunction with our companion guides *South Snowdonia by Car* and *North Snowdonia by Car* — in fact, our routes on Maps 9 and 10 interlink with the Map 7 route described in the North Snowdonia guide.

We have tried to take you within reach of all the favourite beaches and attractive coves, and to show you the best of the inland villages and many of the antiquities in the countryside. Our routes vary in length from nearly 100 miles for the Main Circle Route down to 26 miles for Route E: other variations can be devised by using link roads shown in the Route Directions and Maps — and you can, of course, join each Route at any convenient point.

HOW TO USE YOUR BOOK ON THE ROUTE

Each double page makes up a complete picture of the country ahead of you. On the left you will find a one mile to the inch strip map, with the route marked by a series of dashes. Direction is always from top to bottom so that the map may be looked at in conjunction with the 'directions to driver', with which it is cross-referenced by a letter itemising each major junction point. This enables the driver to have exact guidance every time an opportunity for changing direction occurs, even if it is only 'keep straight, not left'.

With mileage intervals shown, the driver should even have warning when to expect these 'moments of decision', and if a sign exists we have used this to help you, with a 'Follow Sign Marked' column. However, signs may be damaged or defaced, and a re-signing programme is now in progress, which may lead to differences of signing in some cases — so beware of freshly erected signs.

We have also included a description of the towns and villages through which you will pass, together with some photographs to illustrate the route.

To enjoy your journeys to the full be prepared to leave the car as often as you can. There are many coastal footpaths, although not all are clearly marked. Some of the hills can easily be climbed from points described in the route direction — you will be rewarded by breathtaking views. Above all do not attempt to cover too much ground in one day; drive slowly, stop often, and give yourself time to enjoy the beauty of this unspoilt region of North Wales.

COMPILED BY JIM TITCHMARSH
PHOTOGRAPHY BY ALAN AND JIM TITCHMARSH
SERIES EDITOR PETER TITCHMARSH

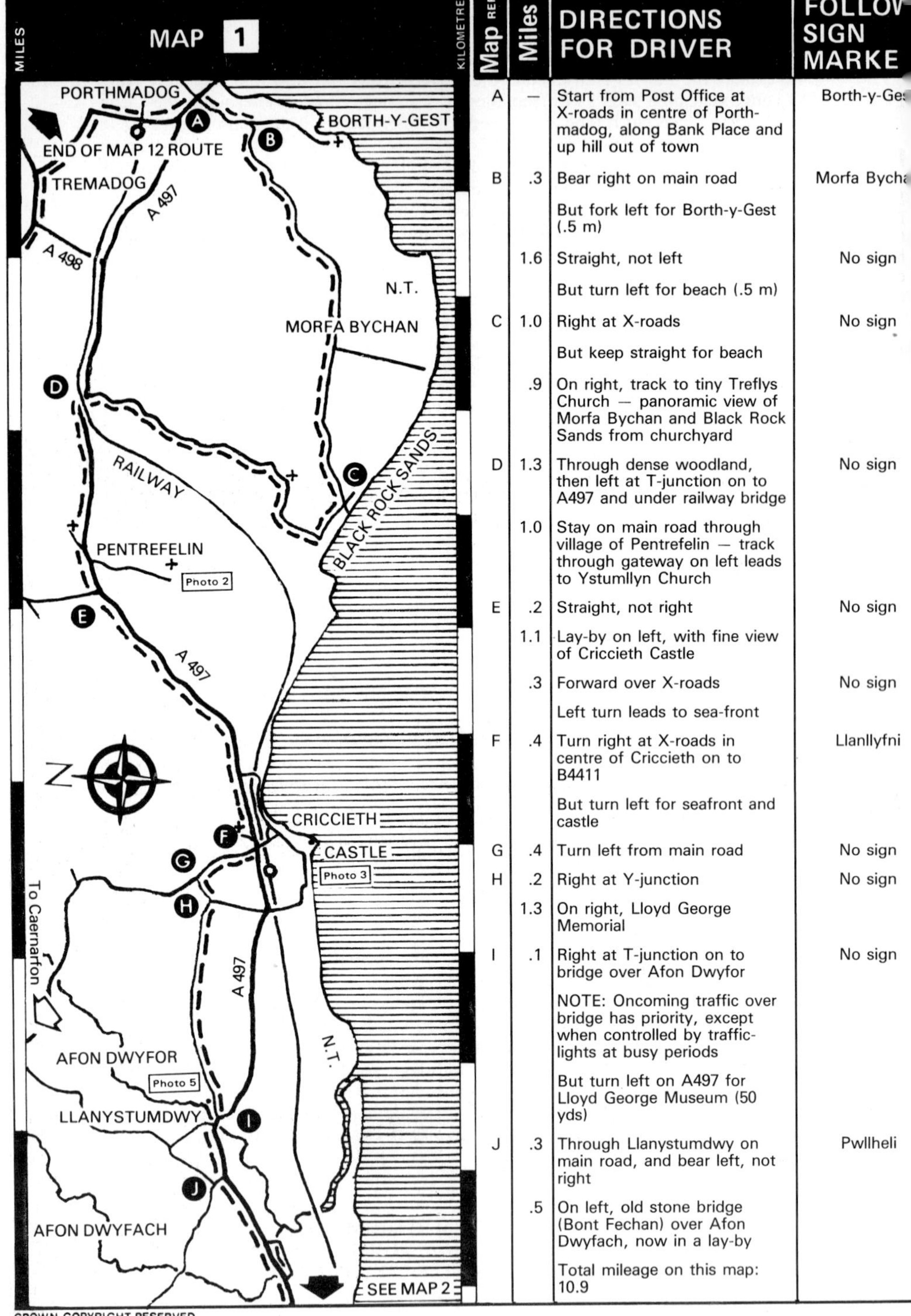

Map REF	Miles	DIRECTIONS FOR DRIVER	FOLLOW SIGN MARKED
A	—	Start from Post Office at X-roads in centre of Porthmadog, along Bank Place and up hill out of town	Borth-y-Gest
B	.3	Bear right on main road	Morfa Bychan
		But fork left for Borth-y-Gest (.5 m)	
	1.6	Straight, not left	No sign
		But turn left for beach (.5 m)	
C	1.0	Right at X-roads	No sign
		But keep straight for beach	
	.9	On right, track to tiny Treflys Church — panoramic view of Morfa Bychan and Black Rock Sands from churchyard	
D	1.3	Through dense woodland, then left at T-junction on to A497 and under railway bridge	No sign
	1.0	Stay on main road through village of Pentrefelin — track through gateway on left leads to Ystumllyn Church	
E	.2	Straight, not right	No sign
	1.1	Lay-by on left, with fine view of Criccieth Castle	
	.3	Forward over X-roads	No sign
		Left turn leads to sea-front	
F	.4	Turn right at X-roads in centre of Criccieth on to B4411	Llanllyfni
		But turn left for seafront and castle	
G	.4	Turn left from main road	No sign
H	.2	Right at Y-junction	No sign
	1.3	On right, Lloyd George Memorial	
I	.1	Right at T-junction on to bridge over Afon Dwyfor	No sign
		NOTE: Oncoming traffic over bridge has priority, except when controlled by traffic-lights at busy periods	
		But turn left on A497 for Lloyd George Museum (50 yds)	
J	.3	Through Llanystumdwy on main road, and bear left, not right	Pwllheli
	.5	On left, old stone bridge (Bont Fechan) over Afon Dwyfach, now in a lay-by	
		Total mileage on this map: 10.9	

Porthmadog (See page 25)

Borth-y-Gest

Less than a mile from the centre of Porthmadog, Borth-y-Gest is a quiet resort, with a sandy harbour full of small yachts, and a fine view across the estuary towards Portmeirion and Harlech. From the car park beside the harbour it is only a short walk past the church overlooking the sea from the headland to several attractive sandy beaches.

Morfa Bychan

This is a modern development of bungalows and caravan sites behind the famous Black Rock Sands — more than a mile of firm clean sand on which you may safely drive your car; two access points are shown in the route directions. Here also is the Porthmadog Golf Club's course, laid out on linksland which is mainly National Trust property.

Pentrefelin

The simple modern church designed by Clough Williams Ellis will be found in the trees on your right behind the petrol station; this replaced the early-Victorian Ystumllyn Church which now moulders away at the end of a farm track, half a mile from the main road. On the south side of the road, near the centre of the village, is a standing stone, which is surely the tallest and slimmest in Wales.

Criccieth

Unspoilt by sea-front shops and 'amusements', Criccieth is a quietly attractive resort, dominated by the Castle ruins on a theatrical mound. To the east of the Castle a gracefully curving promenade surrounds a shallow bay with sand and shingle beach; to the west a simple Marine Parade of Victorian hotels and guest houses. The town centre, with its well-kept green, has a village atmosphere. There is a Victorian parish church (on right of main road, before Point F); a turning to the right, also just before Point F, leads up hill past an older and less pretentious church towards the golf course on the slopes of Mynydd Ednyfed — worth exploring for the panoramic views.

The Castle was built in the time of Llewellyn the Great (early 13c), and strengthened and extended by the English after Edward I had conquered the district in 1284. The English occupation continued fairly peacefully until the reign of Henry IV, when in spite of repairs to the Castle and reinforcement of the garrison, it fell to the Welsh during the rising inspired by Owain Glyndwr, and was burnt and left derelict. Since the 1930's it has been excavated and restored. As usual the official guide is excellent, and tells the whole interesting story.

Llanystumdwy (See Page 5)

1. Porthmadog Harbour

2. Ystumllyn Church

3. Marine Parade, Criccieth

4. Lloyd George Statue,

5. Lloyd George Memorial, Llanystumdwy

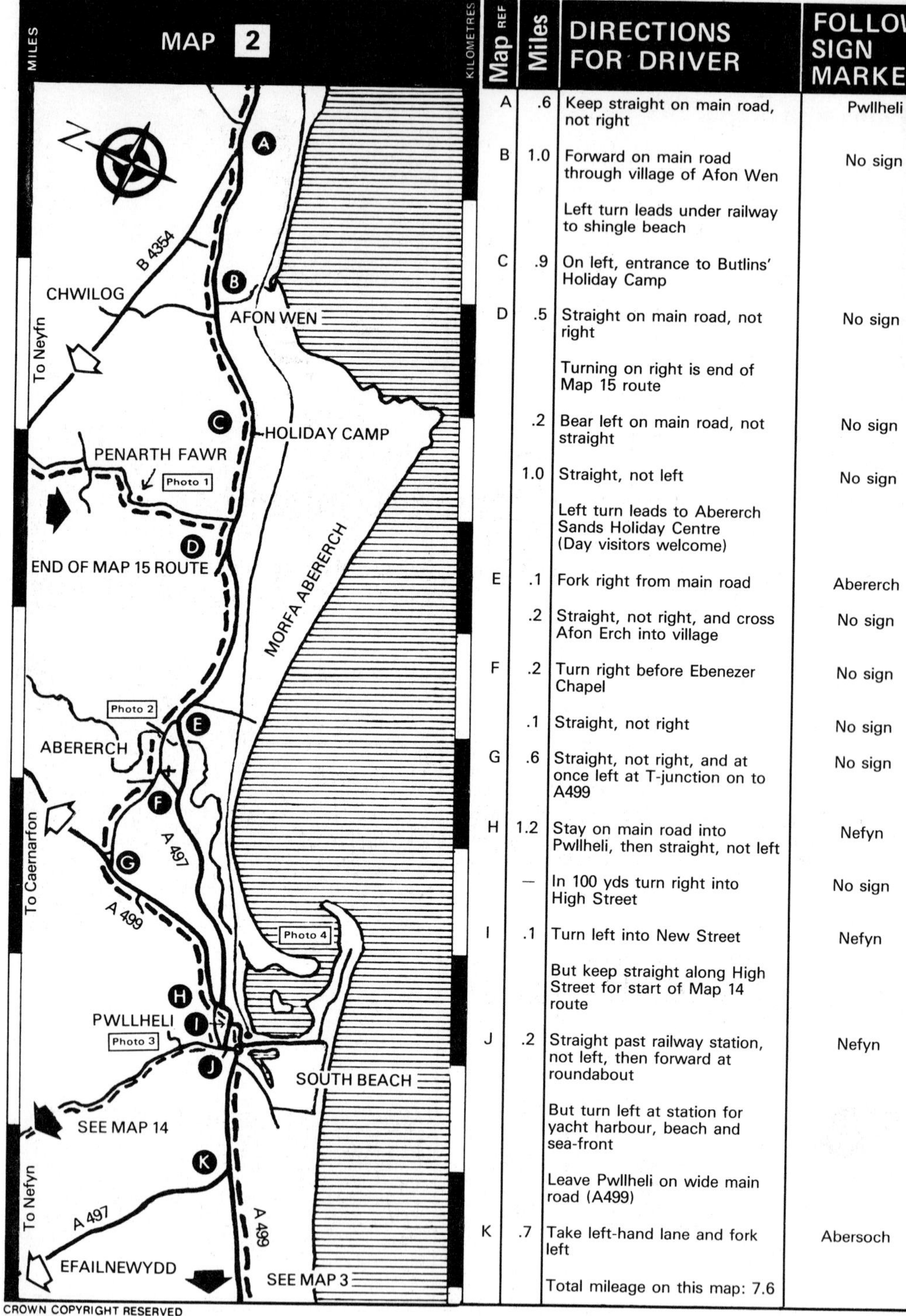

Map REF	Miles	DIRECTIONS FOR DRIVER	FOLLOW SIGN MARKE
A	.6	Keep straight on main road, not right	Pwllheli
B	1.0	Forward on main road through village of Afon Wen	No sign
		Left turn leads under railway to shingle beach	
C	.9	On left, entrance to Butlins' Holiday Camp	
D	.5	Straight on main road, not right	No sign
		Turning on right is end of Map 15 route	
	.2	Bear left on main road, not straight	No sign
	1.0	Straight, not left	No sign
		Left turn leads to Abererch Sands Holiday Centre (Day visitors welcome)	
E	.1	Fork right from main road	Abererch
	.2	Straight, not right, and cross Afon Erch into village	No sign
F	.2	Turn right before Ebenezer Chapel	No sign
	.1	Straight, not right	No sign
G	.6	Straight, not right, and at once left at T-junction on to A499	No sign
H	1.2	Stay on main road into Pwllheli, then straight, not left	Nefyn
	—	In 100 yds turn right into High Street	No sign
I	.1	Turn left into New Street	Nefyn
		But keep straight along High Street for start of Map 14 route	
J	.2	Straight past railway station, not left, then forward at roundabout	Nefyn
		But turn left at station for yacht harbour, beach and sea-front	
		Leave Pwllheli on wide main road (A499)	
K	.7	Take left-hand lane and fork left	Abersoch
		Total mileage on this map: 7.6	

Llanystumdwy (See Map 1)

The name means 'the church at the bend of the Dwy river', and the river, the Afon Dwyfor, is very much in evidence, as the narrow stone bridge in the centre of the village causes severe congestion at busy times. Llanystumdwy is best known for its associations with David Lloyd George, 1st Earl of Dwyfor, who spent his childhood with his widowed mother in a cottage opposite the Feathers Inn. His uncle, the village shoemaker, had his workshop next door. David Lloyd George became a solicitor, and practiced in Manchester and in partnership with his brother in Porthmadog; he was first elected to Parliament as the member for Caernarfon Boroughs in 1890. For many years his home was a house called Brynawelon at Criccieth, and his grave and memorial are at Llanystumdwy.

The memorial, an attractive circular composition in dark grey stone, and the entrance gates to the Museum opposite, were designed by Clough Williams Ellis. The woods in which the memorial stands slope steeply down to the Dywfor, and a footpath beside the river makes a beautiful walk. The Lloyd George Memorial Museum contains many mementoes of the famous politician.

Penarth Fawr (See Page 31)

Abererch

This is a quietly attractive grey and white village, with some unobtrusive modern development, on the banks of the Afon Erch. A restored medieval church and the red and white Ebenezer Chapel face each other at the top of the village (Point F). A turning to the left from the main road before you come to the village leads to the Abererch Sands Holiday Centre, a caravan site in the dunes behind the enormous beach of Morfa Abererch.

Pwllheli

There is little to remind you of the sea as you enter Pwllheli, the busy market centre of the Lleyn, and still a railway terminus. There are only one or two good buildings in the old town; of the many chapels the best is 'Penlan', and the parish church was built in the 'early decorated' style in 1887. But take the wide road past the station entrance, and in half a mile you will come to South Beach, a wide promenade behind a long shingle beach. If you turn left just before reaching the promenade, and drive another half mile through a council estate, you will come to the yacht harbour, with a busy boatyard, and a neat caravan site. Nearby stands the Gimblet Rock, an imposing mass of stone, but much reduced from its original size by quarrying. At one time Pwllheli harbour was busy with trading vessels, but it slowly silted up; in 1903 it was cleared with the help of a Government grant of £70,000, and it is now a popular yachting base.

1. Penarth Fawr

2. Abererch

3. In Pwllheli

4. Pwllheli Harbour

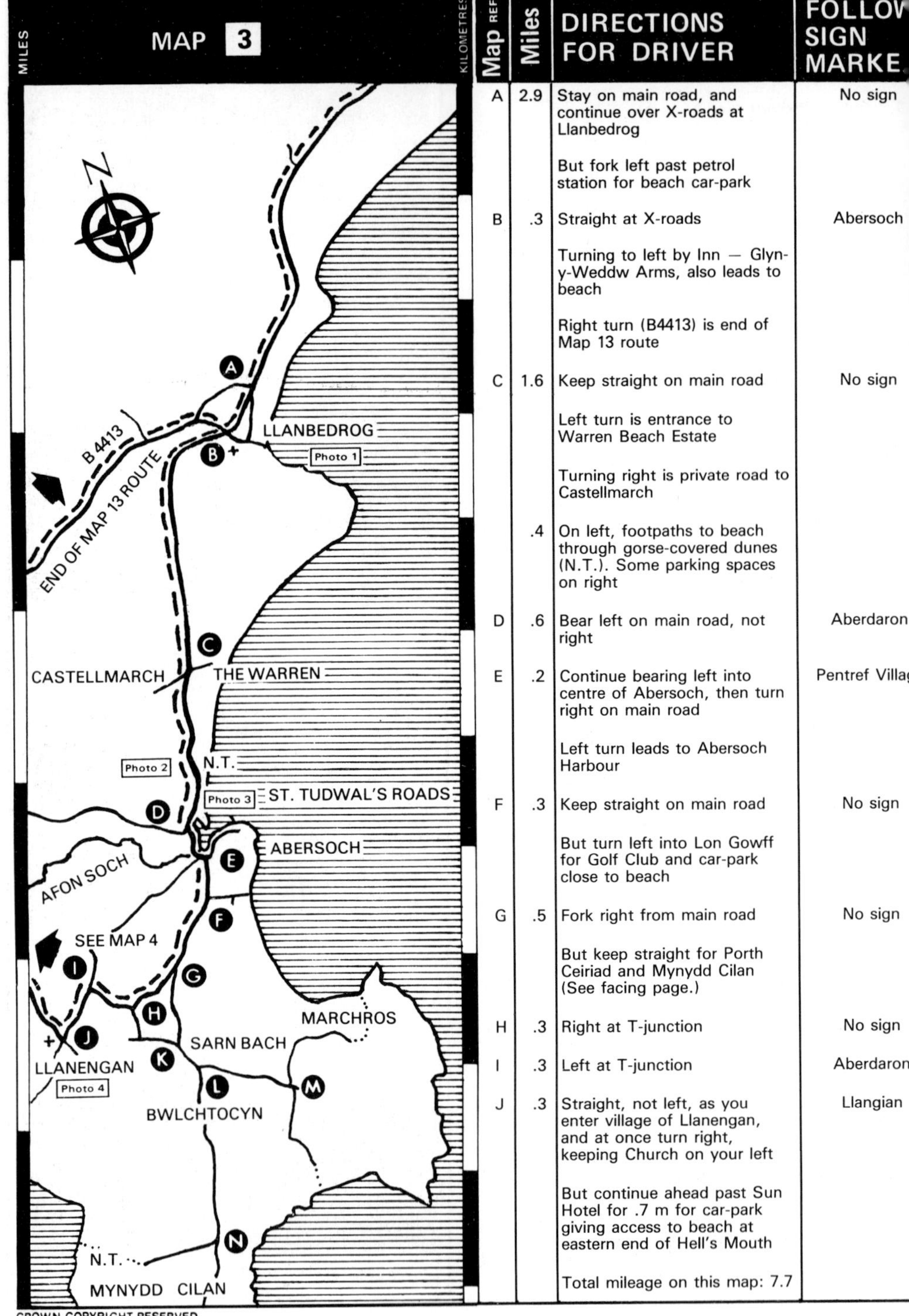

Map Ref	Miles	DIRECTIONS FOR DRIVER	FOLLOW SIGN MARKED
A	2.9	Stay on main road, and continue over X-roads at Llanbedrog	No sign
		But fork left past petrol station for beach car-park	
B	.3	Straight at X-roads	Abersoch
		Turning to left by Inn — Glyn-y-Weddw Arms, also leads to beach	
		Right turn (B4413) is end of Map 13 route	
C	1.6	Keep straight on main road	No sign
		Left turn is entrance to Warren Beach Estate	
		Turning right is private road to Castellmarch	
	.4	On left, footpaths to beach through gorse-covered dunes (N.T.). Some parking spaces on right	
D	.6	Bear left on main road, not right	Aberdaron
E	.2	Continue bearing left into centre of Abersoch, then turn right on main road	Pentref Village
		Left turn leads to Abersoch Harbour	
F	.3	Keep straight on main road	No sign
		But turn left into Lon Gowff for Golf Club and car-park close to beach	
G	.5	Fork right from main road	No sign
		But keep straight for Porth Ceiriad and Mynydd Cilan (See facing page.)	
H	.3	Right at T-junction	No sign
I	.3	Left at T-junction	Aberdaron
J	.3	Straight, not left, as you enter village of Llanengan, and at once turn right, keeping Church on your left	Llangian
		But continue ahead past Sun Hotel for .7 m for car-park giving access to beach at eastern end of Hell's Mouth	
		Total mileage on this map: 7.7	

PLACES OF INTEREST ON THE ROUTE

Llandbedrog

Apart from one or two 17th century cottages nestling at the foot of the tree-covered headland of Mynydd Tirycwmwd, and the much restored little church with its tiny lych gate, the seaward portion of Llandbedrog, almost hidden in the trees between the main road and the sea, is entirely modern. The wide sandy beach is sheltered by the headland from the south-west, and the sands extend eastwards·almost unbroken to Pwllheli. The old village straggles up the hill above the village along B4413 towards Mynytho.

Abersoch

Safe moorings for hundreds of yachts, and the boatyards to service them, explain the growing popularity of Abersoch with sailing folk; others are attracted by the very fine sandy beaches and the sporting golf course. The tidy complex of bungalows and caravans at the Warren has its own shops and services; the beach is long, wide and clean, and day visitors are welcome. The same beach can also be reached by footpaths across National Trust land nearer the village. Standing back from the road opposite the entrance to the Warren is the Jacobean manor house of Castellmarch (private). The other main beach is backed by the golf course, and is easily reached from Point F.

Sarn Bach, Bwlchtocyn, Porth Ceiriad and Mynydd Cilan

The complex of lanes southwards from Point G is well worth exploring, and there are several parking places which give access to the coast. Keep straight, not right, at Point G, and in .5 m keep straight again through the hamlet of Sarn Bach at Point K (see map). At Point L (.2 m) you can turn left (sign Marchros), and left again at Point M (.5 m) — this will take you to the southern end of the main Abersoch beach. The right turn at Point M leads to a car park at Pant Farm, from which it is a short walk to Porth Ceiriad, with a fine beach and spectacular cliff scenery.

If you keep straight at Point L through Bwlchtocyn, in 1 mile at Point N there is a right turn (sign Mynydd Cilan) leading to open moorland (N.T.) which stretches as far as the rocky coast overlooking the south-eastern end of Porth Neigwl. Straight on from Point N takes you to the southern headlands of Trwyn Cilan and Trwyn Llech-y-doll.

Llanengan

The fine parish church dates from the 15th and early 16th centuries. The three bells bear 17th century dates, and are believed to have come from the Abbey of St. Mair on Bardsey, with which Llanengan was traditionally associated; it is no doubt a point of call for Bardsey pilgrims. In the church there is a beautiful screen between nave and chancel, and an offertory chest carved from a single baulk of timber, known as Cyff Engan.

The Sun Hotel is a pleasant free house; in .7 mile down the road past the inn you will find a car park from which a footpath leads to the beach at the south-eastern end of Porth Neigwl (see page 9).

1. Trwyn Llanbedrog

2. Abersoch

3. Abersoch — Mouth of Afon Soch

4. Llanengan Church

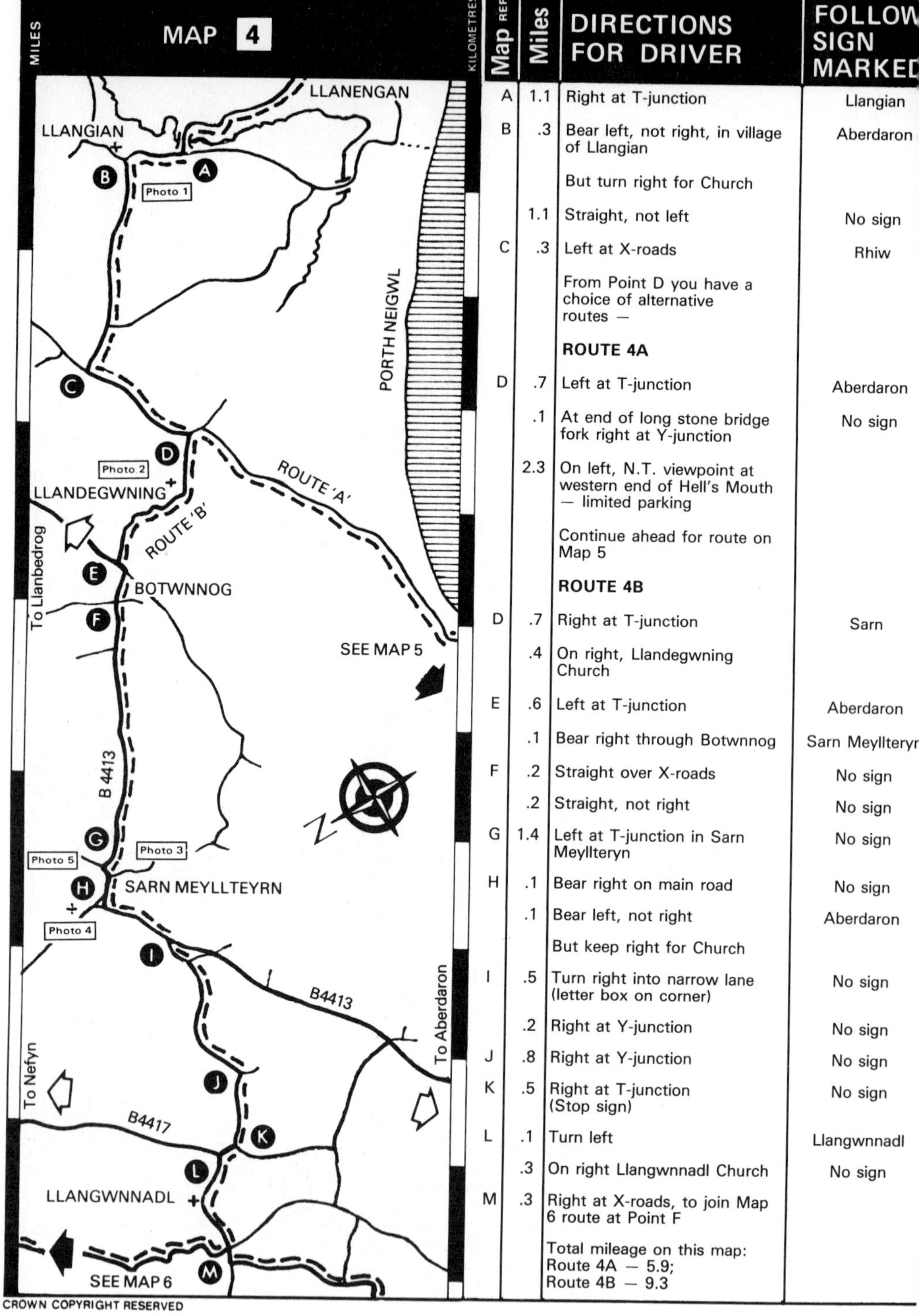

Map REF	Miles	DIRECTIONS FOR DRIVER	FOLLOW SIGN MARKED
A	1.1	Right at T-junction	Llangian
B	.3	Bear left, not right, in village of Llangian	Aberdaron
		But turn right for Church	
	1.1	Straight, not left	No sign
C	.3	Left at X-roads	Rhiw
		From Point D you have a choice of alternative routes —	
		ROUTE 4A	
D	.7	Left at T-junction	Aberdaron
	.1	At end of long stone bridge fork right at Y-junction	No sign
	2.3	On left, N.T. viewpoint at western end of Hell's Mouth — limited parking	
		Continue ahead for route on Map 5	
		ROUTE 4B	
D	.7	Right at T-junction	Sarn
	.4	On right, Llandegwning Church	
E	.6	Left at T-junction	Aberdaron
	.1	Bear right through Botwnnog	Sarn Meyllteryn
F	.2	Straight over X-roads	No sign
	.2	Straight, not right	No sign
G	1.4	Left at T-junction in Sarn Meyllteryn	No sign
H	.1	Bear right on main road	No sign
	.1	Bear left, not right	Aberdaron
		But keep right for Church	
I	.5	Turn right into narrow lane (letter box on corner)	No sign
	.2	Right at Y-junction	No sign
J	.8	Right at Y-junction	No sign
K	.5	Right at T-junction (Stop sign)	No sign
L	.1	Turn left	Llangwnnadl
	.3	On right Llangwnnadl Church	No sign
M	.3	Right at X-roads, to join Map 6 route at Point F	
		Total mileage on this map: Route 4A — 5.9; Route 4B — 9.3	

Porth Neigwl (Hell's Mouth)

This great bay, with 3½ miles of almost deserted sand, has a horrid reputation from the days of sail when the combination of south-westerly gales and treacherous offshore currents claimed many victims. Today it looks harmless enough, particularly when the sun shines. For the motorist the best access point for the beach is near Llanengan (see page 7).

Llangian

Some years ago Llangian earned the title of 'Best Kept Village in Wales', and that standard is still maintained, with spruce cottages and colourful gardens. The simple church, dating from the 13th and 15th centuries, with some modern addition, has a particular treasure in the churchyard. This is a rough stone pillar with a Latin inscription saying that the remains of 'Melius the doctor, son of Martinus, lie here'. It dates from the 5th or 6th century A.D., and is the only record in Britain of an early Christian burial which mentions the deceased's profession.

Llandegwning

There is hardly any village — just a charming miniature church with a conical spire, set on a small tower which is octagonal below and round above.

Sarn Meyllteryn

Pleasantly sited in a wooded valley, this village boasts three inns — the Penlan Hotel and the Penrhyn Arms on the main road, and the whitewashed Ty-Newydd Inn on the hillside to the left of our route. No doubt it was once a more important place than it is now. The sharply-pointed church (mid-19th century) has a beautiful position overlooking the valley on the side road from Point H.

'Arthur's Quoit' and Penllech Church

The best way to visit Cefnamwlch Burial Chamber (popularly known as 'Arthur's Quoit'), and the old Penllech Church, is to continue from Point H past Sarn Meyllteryn Church. In 1.2 m you will see the stones which formed the framework of the Iron Age burial chamber in a field to your left. In a further .3 m turn left on to B4417; then in another .2 m you will see a farm track on the right which leads to the church, now neglected and alone except for the adjacent farmyard. Another 1.2 m forward on B4417 brings you to cross-roads (Point L), where you turn right to rejoin our route.

Llangwnnadl

Again there is no obvious village, but this unusual three-aisled church is still active and well cared-for. Spacious and airy, it was built in the 15th and 16th centuries on the site of a 6th century church. The sanctuary bell is a reproduction of the original 16th century bell now in the Cardiff Museum. In the south wall there is a 6th century stone with an inscribed Celtic cross, said to be the headstone of the founder's grave.

1. Cottages at Llangian

2. Llandegwning Church

3. Ty-Newydd Inn, Sarn Meyllteryn

4. Sarn Meyllteryn Church

5. Penrhyn Arms Hotel, Sarn Meyllteryn

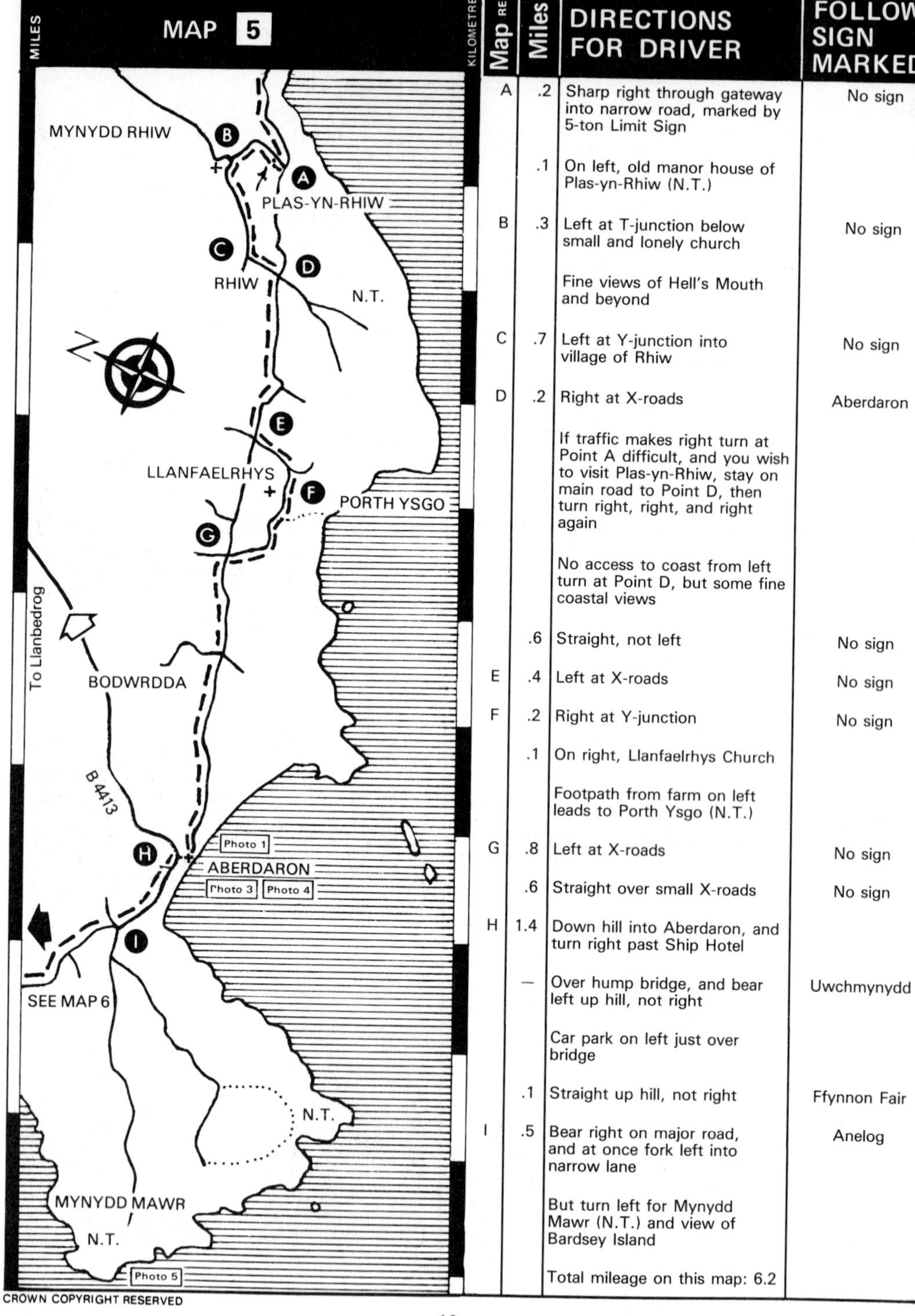

KILOMETRES	Map REF	Miles	DIRECTIONS FOR DRIVER	FOLLOW SIGN MARKED
	A	.2	Sharp right through gateway into narrow road, marked by 5-ton Limit Sign	No sign
		.1	On left, old manor house of Plas-yn-Rhiw (N.T.)	
	B	.3	Left at T-junction below small and lonely church	No sign
			Fine views of Hell's Mouth and beyond	
	C	.7	Left at Y-junction into village of Rhiw	No sign
	D	.2	Right at X-roads	Aberdaron
			If traffic makes right turn at Point A difficult, and you wish to visit Plas-yn-Rhiw, stay on main road to Point D, then turn right, right, and right again	
			No access to coast from left turn at Point D, but some fine coastal views	
		.6	Straight, not left	No sign
	E	.4	Left at X-roads	No sign
	F	.2	Right at Y-junction	No sign
		.1	On right, Llanfaelrhys Church	
			Footpath from farm on left leads to Porth Ysgo (N.T.)	
	G	.8	Left at X-roads	No sign
		.6	Straight over small X-roads	No sign
	H	1.4	Down hill into Aberdaron, and turn right past Ship Hotel	
		—	Over hump bridge, and bear left up hill, not right	Uwchmynydd
			Car park on left just over bridge	
		.1	Straight up hill, not right	Ffynnon Fair
	I	.5	Bear right on major road, and at once fork left into narrow lane	Anelog
			But turn left for Mynydd Mawr (N.T.) and view of Bardsey Island	
			Total mileage on this map: 6.2	

Rhiw

This village on the slopes of Mynydd Rhiw is the highest in the Lleyn. Below the village the 16th century manor house of Plas-yn-Rhiw looks out beyond its beautiful woodland gardens across Porth Neigwl to the distant Welsh hills. It was given to the National Trust by the three daughters of William and Constance Keating in memory of their parents. The house and gardens are open to visitors (see inside rear cover for details). The Misses Keating have also been generous benefactors in giving the National Trust several areas of coastline in the district.

Aberdaron

The most westerly resort of the Lleyn, a village of steep hills, a stream with a medieval hump-back bridge, and a mile-long sheltered beach. Aberdaron was the last stage for pilgrims journeying to the Abbey of St. Mair on Bardsey Island, and their 14th century rest-house 'Y-Gegin Fawr' — 'The Old Kitchen' — is still a cafe. The barn-like church on the edge of the beach dates from the 12th and 15th centuries; it stands on the site of an earlier foundation, and has a well-preserved Norman doorway. Of the more modern buildings, the dignified Post Office was designed by Clough Williams Ellis.

Mynydd Mawr

Turn left at Point I and keep straight for 1½ miles to a gate on to National Trust property which embraces the whole of Mynydd Mawr (Big Mountain) and the headland of Braich-y-Pwll — the 'Land's End' of Wales. A concrete road zig-zags up hill to a car park on the summit from which the views are tremendous — Bardsey Island two miles SSW, and a panorama of the coastline of Lleyn, and the Welsh mainland. Footpaths lead across the rocky moorland to the cliffs, and on the eastern side of the headland it is possible, but dangerous, to scramble down to the shore to find the remains of an ancient church. Here also is Ffynnon Fair (St. Mary's Well), which is said always to yield fresh water, although covered by each tide.

Bardsey Island (Ynys Enlli)

The sound between the mainland and Bardsey Island is a notorious tide-race, and one possible translation of the Welsh name is 'Isle of Tides (or Eddies)'. The English name may have been derived from 'Birdsey'; appropriately the Island is now a bird sanctuary, and is visited mainly by students of bird life and the lighthouse keepers. At one time it supported a small farming and fishing community. Only a ruined tower and a few stones now remain of the ancient Abbey of St. Mair (Mary), which was founded by St. Cadfan in the 6th century. The monks of Bangor-is-Coed, near Chester, came here for refuge when they were expelled by the Saxons, and the Abbey was a place of pilgrimage for hundreds of years. Ancient poets say that 20,000 'saints', or holy men, are buried on the island.

1. Norman Doorway, Aberdaron Church

2. Roman Tombstone, Langian (see p. 9)

3. The Ship Hotel, Aberdaron

4. Y-Gegin Fawr, Aberdaron

5. Bardsey Island

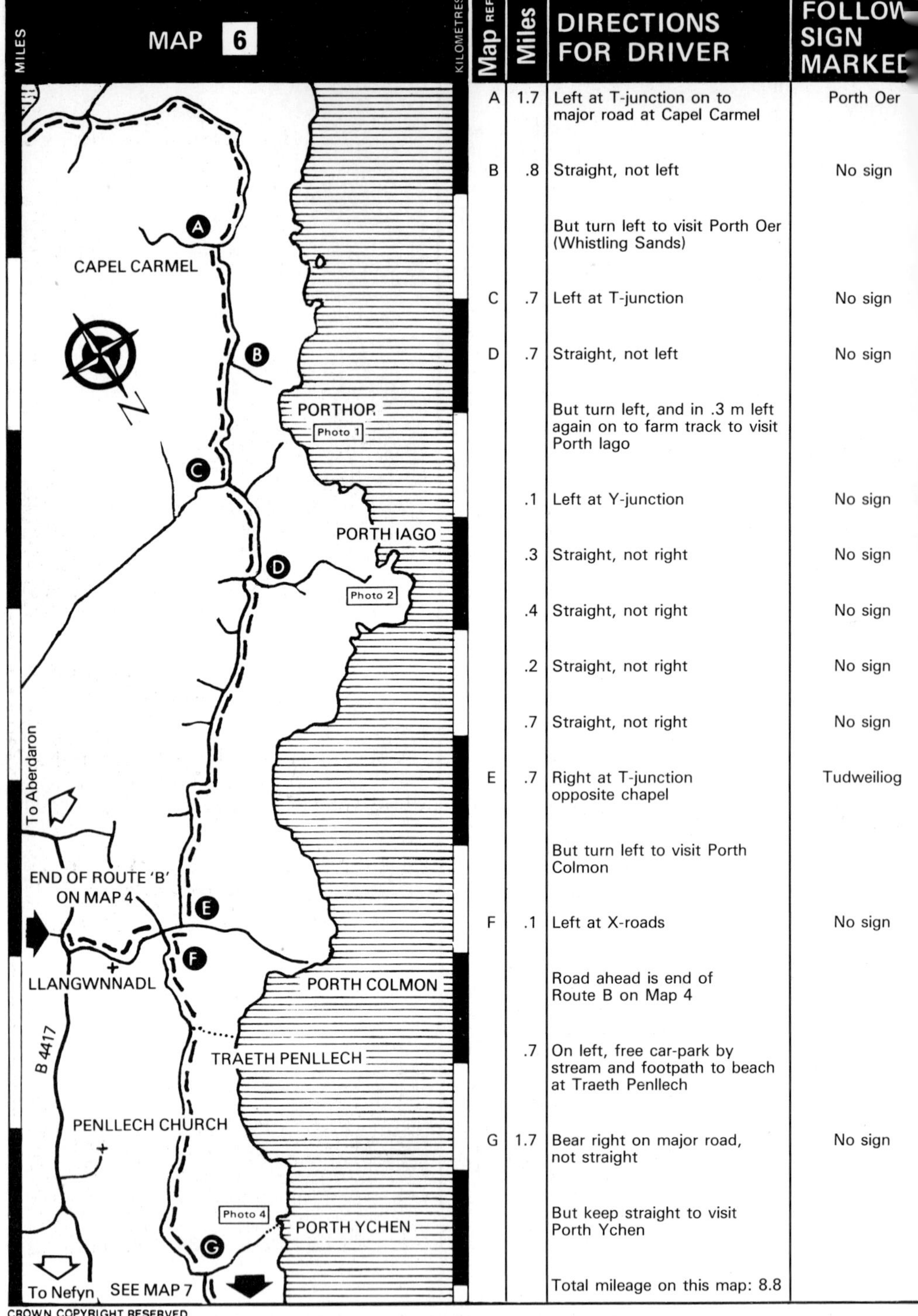

Map REF	Miles	DIRECTIONS FOR DRIVER	FOLLOW SIGN MARKED
A	1.7	Left at T-junction on to major road at Capel Carmel	Porth Oer
B	.8	Straight, not left	No sign
		But turn left to visit Porth Oer (Whistling Sands)	
C	.7	Left at T-junction	No sign
D	.7	Straight, not left	No sign
		But turn left, and in .3 m left again on to farm track to visit Porth Iago	
	.1	Left at Y-junction	No sign
	.3	Straight, not right	No sign
	.4	Straight, not right	No sign
	.2	Straight, not right	No sign
	.7	Straight, not right	No sign
E	.7	Right at T-junction opposite chapel	Tudweiliog
		But turn left to visit Porth Colmon	
F	.1	Left at X-roads	No sign
		Road ahead is end of Route B on Map 4	
	.7	On left, free car-park by stream and footpath to beach at Traeth Penllech	
G	1.7	Bear right on major road, not straight	No sign
		But keep straight to visit Porth Ychen	
		Total mileage on this map: 8.8	

Porthor (or Porth Oer) — Whistling Sands Bay

The sand of the bay is said to produce a whistling sound if it is walked on when dry — hence the popular name. Unfortunately we did not have any chance to test it. Take the turning to the left at Point B; in ¼ mile there is a large car park, from which it is only a short walk down a fairly steep path to the beach.

Porth Iago

This is a delightful spot — a cove barely 100 yards across with a beach of golden sand between rocky headlands. It faces south-west and is a perfect sun-trap. To find it take the left turn at Point D, and in about ¼ mile turn left on to a fairly rough farm track (signed), pay a parking fee at the farm and continue to an ample grass car park just above the beach — less than a mile altogether from the main route.

Port Colmon

A drive of nearly a mile along a good road from Point E brings you to a rocky harbour where you can park. Here you can sit and enjoy the coastal scenery, or walk to your right along the cliff-top to a stretch of sandy beach, which is one end of Traeth Penllech (see below).

Traeth Penllech

About a mile in length, this beach of firm sand can be reached from Porth Colmon, or by a footpath from the car park on our route (see Route Directions). For about ¼ mile the path follows a stream which suddenly cascades down to the sea through the ravine it has cut for itself in the low rocky cliff. There is an easy climb down to the beach.

Porth Ychen

Less than ½ mile down the turning from Point G will be found a group of cottages where there is some parking space (but be careful not to obstruct the residents' entrances). Straight ahead is a footpath across a stretch of gorse and heather covered moorland which leads to a tiny rocky bay with a weed-strewn shingle beach.

Penllech Church (See page 9)

GLOSSARY OF SOME WELSH PLACE NAMES

Aber—a river mouth	Carn, Carnedd—a cairn
Afon—a river	Carreg—stone
Bach—small, little	Cefn—a ridge
Bedd—a grave	Coed—a wood
Betws—a chapel	Craig—a rock or crag
Blaen—the head of a valley	Crib—a ridge or jagged edge
Bont—a bridge	Croes—a cross
Bwlch—pass	Cwm—a hollow or coombe
Bychan—small	Dinas—a natural fortress
Cae—an enclosed field	
Caer—a camp or fortress	Du, Ddu, Dhu—black
	Fach—small
Capel—chapel	Fawr—large

Continued on page 23

1. Porthor — 'The Whistling Sands'

2. Porth Iago

3. 'Arthur's Quoit'

4. Porth Ychen

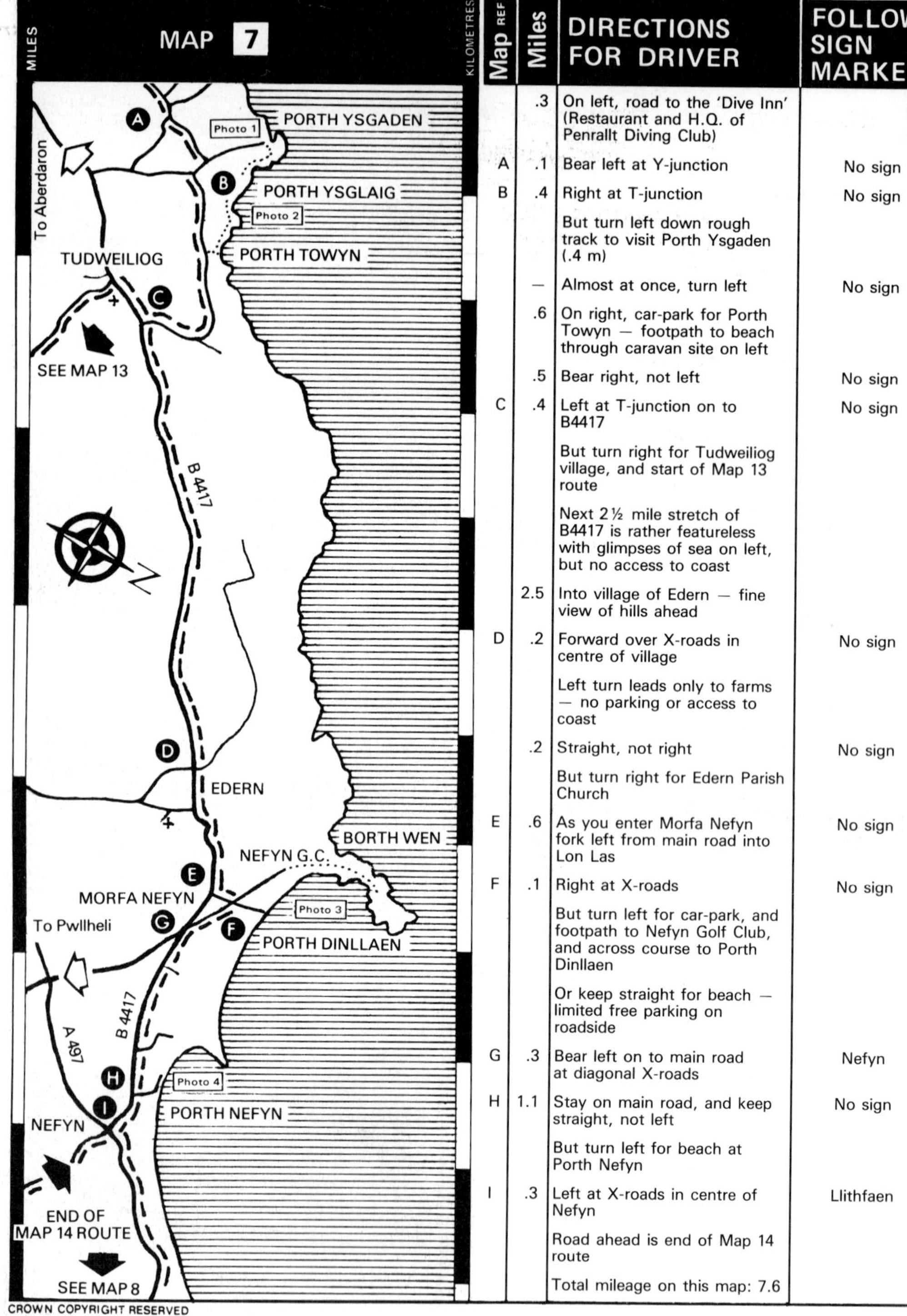

Map REF	Miles	DIRECTIONS FOR DRIVER	FOLLOW SIGN MARKED
	.3	On left, road to the 'Dive Inn' (Restaurant and H.Q. of Penrallt Diving Club)	
A	.1	Bear left at Y-junction	No sign
B	.4	Right at T-junction	No sign
		But turn left down rough track to visit Porth Ysgaden (.4 m)	
—		Almost at once, turn left	No sign
	.6	On right, car-park for Porth Towyn — footpath to beach through caravan site on left	
	.5	Bear right, not left	No sign
C	.4	Left at T-junction on to B4417	No sign
		But turn right for Tudweiliog village, and start of Map 13 route	
		Next 2½ mile stretch of B4417 is rather featureless with glimpses of sea on left, but no access to coast	
	2.5	Into village of Edern — fine view of hills ahead	
D	.2	Forward over X-roads in centre of village	No sign
		Left turn leads only to farms — no parking or access to coast	
	.2	Straight, not right	No sign
		But turn right for Edern Parish Church	
E	.6	As you enter Morfa Nefyn fork left from main road into Lon Las	No sign
F	.1	Right at X-roads	No sign
		But turn left for car-park, and footpath to Nefyn Golf Club, and across course to Porth Dinllaen	
		Or keep straight for beach — limited free parking on roadside	
G	.3	Bear left on to main road at diagonal X-roads	Nefyn
H	1.1	Stay on main road, and keep straight, not left	No sign
		But turn left for beach at Porth Nefyn	
I	.3	Left at X-roads in centre of Nefyn	Llithfaen
		Road ahead is end of Map 14 route	
		Total mileage on this map: 7.6	

Porth Ysgaden

A very rough track to the left from Point B takes you to Porth Ysgaden, known as the 'Herring Harbour', since it was once the base for a local fishing industry. The harbour buildings are now in ruins, but large mooring rings can still be seen on the rocks. A few local crab and lobster fishermen still keep their boats and gear down here. The surrounding coastline is extremely rocky, and it is a wild and dangerous place in a westerly gale. Footpaths eastwards over the cliffs lead to the next cove — Porth Ysglaig — and continue on to Porth Towyn (see below).

Porth Towyn

This is a popular sandy beach, and notices restrict parking in the road nearby, but there is a car park at the farm, from which a short footpath through a caravan site takes you down to the seashore.

Tudweiliog (See page 27)

Morfa Nefyn and Porth Dinllaen

As you approach Morfa Nefyn on the main road, there is nothing to suggest, apart from the name (Morfa means 'bog' or 'sea-marsh') that the sea is anywhere near. In fact the beach known as Porth Dinllaen, more than a mile of firm yellow sand, is only a few hundred yards from Point F. In the shelter of the headland at the western end of the beach is the peaceful hamlet of Porth Dinllaen, which the casual visitor can reach only by walking across the sands from Morfa Nefyn at low tide, or by a footpath across the golf course, which starts from the car park at Point F. Only residents who have a key to the golf course gate may take their cars on to the headland; suitable vehicles can drive over the sands at low tide.

There are traces of an Iron Age promontory fort on the headland. The unique situation of Porth Dinllean makes it a wonderfully peaceful spot, and the houses there are much sought after; there is even a prosperous little inn which hardly provides its patrons with any breathalyser problems. The ubiquitous William Madocks, M.P., of Porthmadog fame, was the author of a scheme to turn Porth Dinllaen into a port for the Irish Mail — thankfully it came to nothing, but not before the almost straight road from the south coast of Lleyn had been specially built to carry the mail traffic.

Porth Nefyn

At the eastern end of Porth Dinllaen the headland of Penrhyn Nefyn separates it from the next bay — Porth Nefyn, another fine sandy beach. This is easily reached by the rather insignificant turning on the left at Point H.

Nefyn (See page 29)

1. Porth Ysgaden

2. Porth Towyn

3. Porth Dinllaen

4. The Rivals from Porth Nefyn

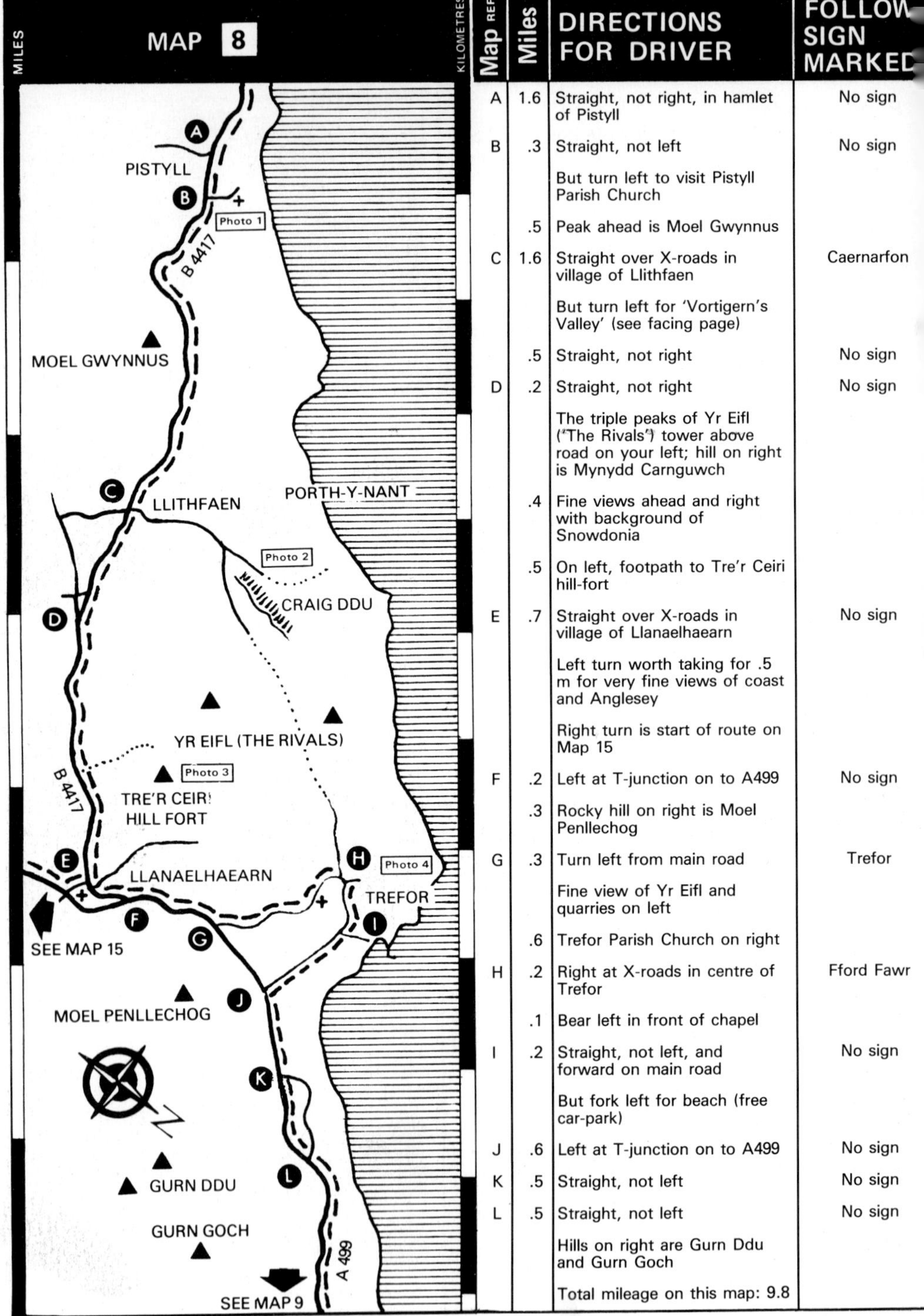

Map REF	Miles	DIRECTIONS FOR DRIVER	FOLLOW SIGN MARKED
A	1.6	Straight, not right, in hamlet of Pistyll	No sign
B	.3	Straight, not left	No sign
		But turn left to visit Pistyll Parish Church	
	.5	Peak ahead is Moel Gwynnus	
C	1.6	Straight over X-roads in village of Llithfaen	Caernarfon
		But turn left for 'Vortigern's Valley' (see facing page)	
	.5	Straight, not right	No sign
D	.2	Straight, not right	No sign
		The triple peaks of Yr Eifl ('The Rivals') tower above road on your left; hill on right is Mynydd Carnguwch	
	.4	Fine views ahead and right with background of Snowdonia	
	.5	On left, footpath to Tre'r Ceiri hill-fort	
E	.7	Straight over X-roads in village of Llanaelhaearn	No sign
		Left turn worth taking for .5 m for very fine views of coast and Anglesey	
		Right turn is start of route on Map 15	
F	.2	Left at T-junction on to A499	No sign
	.3	Rocky hill on right is Moel Penllechog	
G	.3	Turn left from main road	Trefor
		Fine view of Yr Eifl and quarries on left	
	.6	Trefor Parish Church on right	
H	.2	Right at X-roads in centre of Trefor	Fford Fawr
	.1	Bear left in front of chapel	
I	.2	Straight, not left, and forward on main road	No sign
		But fork left for beach (free car-park)	
J	.6	Left at T-junction on to A499	No sign
K	.5	Straight, not left	No sign
L	.5	Straight, not left	No sign
		Hills on right are Gurn Ddu and Gurn Goch	
		Total mileage on this map: 9.8	

Pistyll

The simple rectangular parish church of St. Beuno is at least partly 12th century, but high in the wall by the altar window there is a faint inscription which is thought to be the date 1050. Note the strong buttressing of the west front and the massive roof timbers; it was thatched until about 100 years ago. There are traces of wall paintings and a leper's window. At one time there were only three windows, all in the chancel, which made it very dark inside, but the congregation were no doubt illiterate, and had no need of light for reading. When we called soon after the harvest festival the church was still delightfully filled with the scent of hay and wild flowers strewn on the floor and used for decoration.

Llithfaen

In this exposed hillside village the turning to the left from the cross-roads at Point C leads to 'Vortigern's Valley'. Vortigern was the 'Great Prince' of the 5th century, who summoned Hengist and Horsa to his aid, and is supposed to have died here. In ½ mile you will come to a car park and picnic area (Forestry Commission); do not attempt to drive further, but take the footpath through the plantation on to the high slopes overlooking the sea and a long shingle beach with the remains of an abandoned pier. Behind the beach (Porth-y-Nant) stand the ruins of quarrymen's cottages, which you can reach on foot by a very rough track from the car park. Prominent across the valley is the sheer rock face of Craig Ddu (Black Crag), from which rise the steep slopes of Yr Eifl, scarred with disused quarries.

Yr Eifl — 'The Rivals'

These three peaks are a prominent landmark, with their height somewhat exaggerated by the nearness of the sea and the low ground to the south. Properly the Welsh name means 'The Forks' — 'The Rivals' is a fancy name thought up by the English. The central peak is the highest 564 m (1850 ft), and the one nearest the sea the lowest 444 m (1458 ft), its slopes ending in the rugged headland of Trwyn-y-Gorlech above Porth-y-Nant. The eastern peak above Llanaelhaearn 485 m (1591 ft) is crowned by an ancient hill fort — 'Tre'r Ceiri — to which there is a fairly easy footpath from the main road (see Route Directions). The view from the summit on a clear day is one of the best in Wales, taking in most of the Lleyn, Anglesey and Snowdonia, with even a glimpse of the Isle of Man when conditions are favourable. Tre'r Ceiri is a group of cytiau (hut circles), stone walled structures which were once roofed with poles and bracken. The settlement covered more than 5 acres, and was surrounded by walls which still rise to 15 ft in places.

Llanaelhaearn (See page 31)

Trefor (See page 19)

1. St. Beuno's Church, Pistyll

2. Vortigern's Valley

3. Tre'r Ceiri Hill Fort

4. Yr Eifl from Trefor

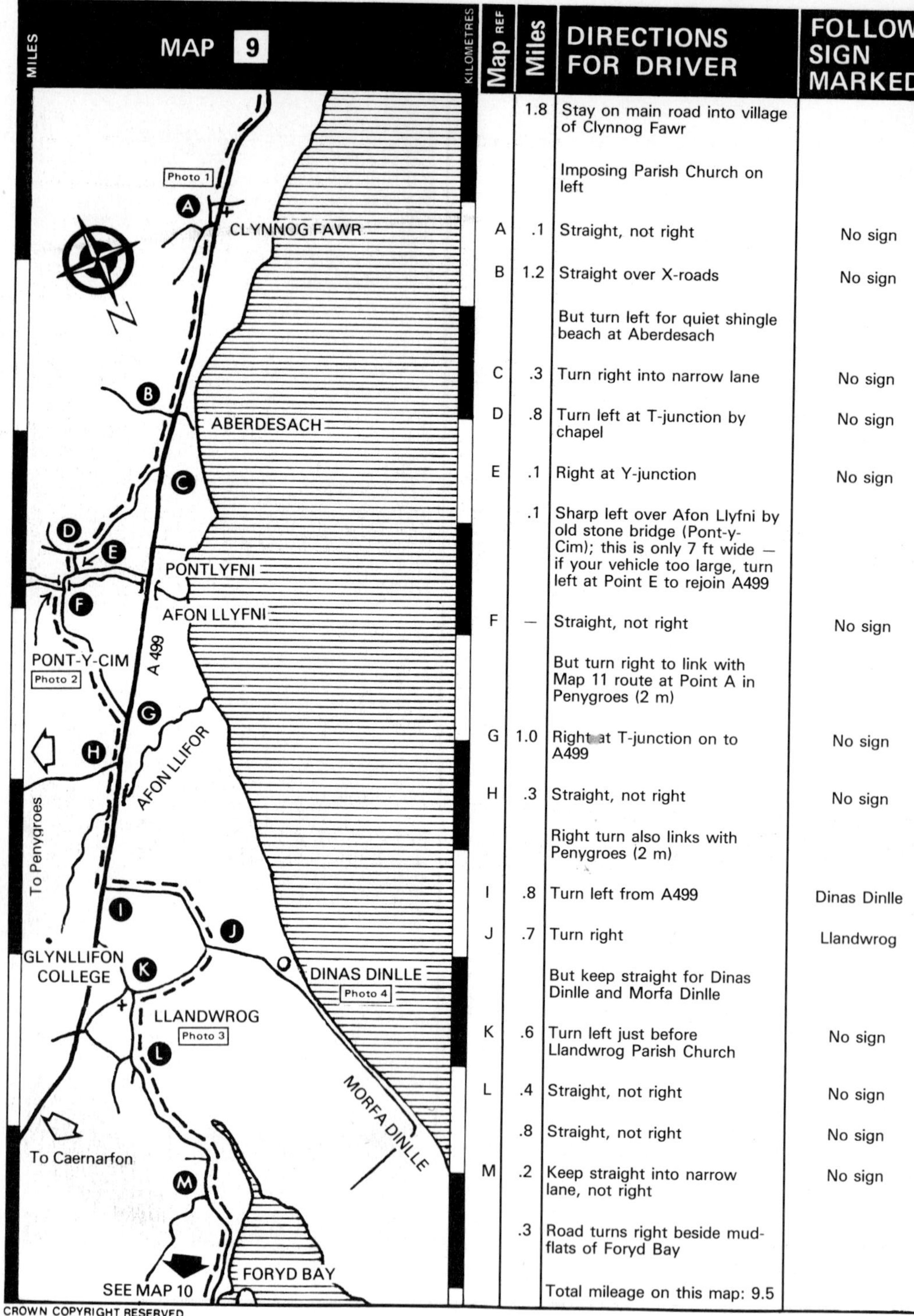

Map REF	Miles	DIRECTIONS FOR DRIVER	FOLLOW SIGN MARKED
	1.8	Stay on main road into village of Clynnog Fawr	
		Imposing Parish Church on left	
A	.1	Straight, not right	No sign
B	1.2	Straight over X-roads	No sign
		But turn left for quiet shingle beach at Aberdesach	
C	.3	Turn right into narrow lane	No sign
D	.8	Turn left at T-junction by chapel	No sign
E	.1	Right at Y-junction	No sign
	.1	Sharp left over Afon Llyfni by old stone bridge (Pont-y-Cim); this is only 7 ft wide — if your vehicle too large, turn left at Point E to rejoin A499	
F	—	Straight, not right	No sign
		But turn right to link with Map 11 route at Point A in Penygroes (2 m)	
G	1.0	Right at T-junction on to A499	No sign
H	.3	Straight, not right	No sign
		Right turn also links with Penygroes (2 m)	
I	.8	Turn left from A499	Dinas Dinlle
J	.7	Turn right	Llandwrog
		But keep straight for Dinas Dinlle and Morfa Dinlle	
K	.6	Turn left just before Llandwrog Parish Church	No sign
L	.4	Straight, not right	No sign
	.8	Straight, not right	No sign
M	.2	Keep straight into narrow lane, not right	No sign
	.3	Road turns right beside mud-flats of Foryd Bay	
		Total mileage on this map: 9.5	

Trefor (See Map 8)

Many of the typical quarrymen's cottages have been refurbished as holiday homes, and are gay with new paint. The quarries themselves on the slopes of Yr Eifl to the west of the village, and Gurn Ddu to the east have declined, and the pier from which the stone was loaded on to coasters is derelict. The beach at Trefor is mainly mud and shingle, but there are patches of sand.

Clynnog Fawr

The magnificent late Perpendicular church dedicated to St. Beuno was built as a collegiate church not later than the reign of the Tudor Henry VIII on the site of an earlier building. St. Beuno, probably the most important Welsh saint after St. David, came to Clynnog towards the end of his life in AD 635. The vast interior has the feeling of a cathedral, and contains some fine examples of wood carving in the roof timbers, rood screen and misericord seats. Relics include a massive oaken strong-box known as 'The Chest of Beuno', and a pair of dog-tongs. The holy water of St. Beuno's Well, on the side of the main road about 300 yards south-west of the church, was said to cure all ills. Just visible from the main road, and close to the sea on private ground, there is a fine cromlech or burial chamber.

Pont-y-Cim

The ancient single-span bridge once carried the main route from Caernarfon into the Lleyn, but long ago was by-passed by the main road through Pontlyfni. The bridge carries the date 1612, and is only 7 ft wide between parapets — just enough for a private car. It spans the Afon Llyfni which yields good salmon and trout fishing. Pontlyfni has some seaside bungalows and caravans, but the beach is stony and often covered with strong smelling sea-weed.

Llandwrog

A Gothic village built by Lord Newborough in the 1830's; the church with an impressive spire and a Gothic revival interior dates from 1860 — there are some beautiful monuments in the Wynne Chapel near the altar. In the village close to the church is a group of almshouses set in an attractive curve.

Dinas Dinlle

On this mound by the sea were some early British defence works; the Romans came and built a fort with double ramparts, and a causeway to connect it with Segontium, their base at Caernarfon — in fact it formed the seaward end of Watling Street, the trunk route which was vital for the military control of the country. Nearby a few modern bungalows, cafes and guest houses show little respect for history. A dead straight road continues northwards for more than a mile beside the lonely shingle beach to the remains of a war-time airfield.

1. St. Beuno's Church, Clynnog Fawr

2. Pont-y-Cim

3. Almshouses at Llandwrog

4. Yr Eifl from Dinas Dinlle

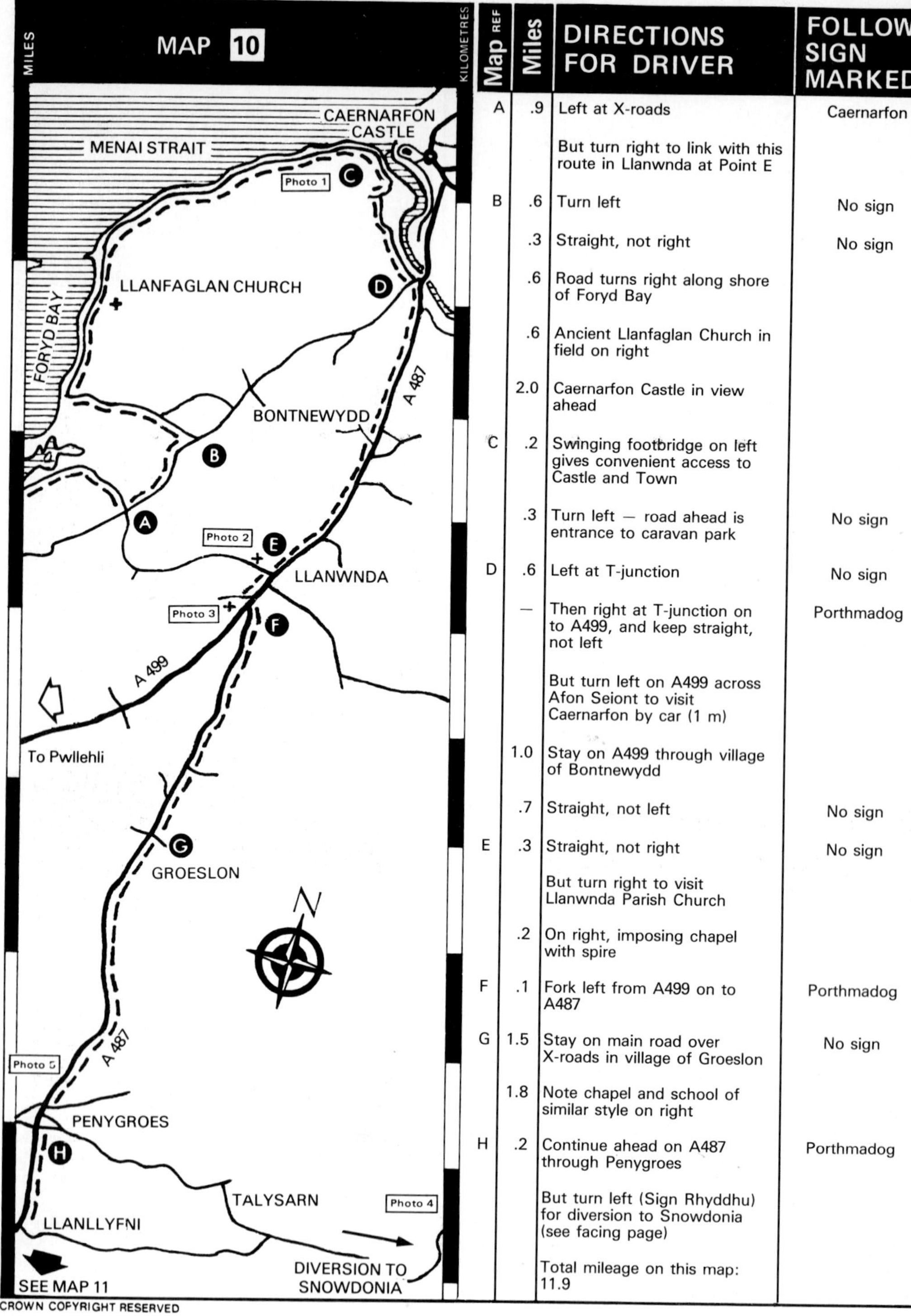

Map REF	Miles	DIRECTIONS FOR DRIVER	FOLLOW SIGN MARKED
A	.9	Left at X-roads	Caernarfon
		But turn right to link with this route in Llanwnda at Point E	
B	.6	Turn left	No sign
	.3	Straight, not right	No sign
	.6	Road turns right along shore of Foryd Bay	
	.6	Ancient Llanfaglan Church in field on right	
	2.0	Caernarfon Castle in view ahead	
C	.2	Swinging footbridge on left gives convenient access to Castle and Town	
	.3	Turn left — road ahead is entrance to caravan park	No sign
D	.6	Left at T-junction	No sign
	—	Then right at T-junction on to A499, and keep straight, not left	Porthmadog
		But turn left on A499 across Afon Seiont to visit Caernarfon by car (1 m)	
	1.0	Stay on A499 through village of Bontnewydd	
	.7	Straight, not left	No sign
E	.3	Straight, not right	No sign
		But turn right to visit Llanwnda Parish Church	
	.2	On right, imposing chapel with spire	
F	.1	Fork left from A499 on to A487	Porthmadog
G	1.5	Stay on main road over X-roads in village of Groeslon	No sign
	1.8	Note chapel and school of similar style on right	
H	.2	Continue ahead on A487 through Penygroes	Porthmadog
		But turn left (Sign Rhyddhu) for diversion to Snowdonia (see facing page)	
		Total mileage on this map: 11.9	

Llanfaglan Church

The community once served by this medieval church has gone, and it now stands alone, sheltered by trees within the churchyard wall and surrounded by open fields. It escaped the restoring zeal of the 19th century, but is still in good repair, and used for the occasional service and burial. The lintel inside the door is a late Roman tombstone, and there are other Roman stones in the walls — evidence that this site was a place of worship long before the present building.

Caernarfon

The unobstructed view of Edward I's finest castle across the Afon Seiont fully justifies our detour along the shore of the Menai Strait. Once there was a toll-bridge across the river, but this was burned down; more recently a swinging footbridge has been built and you can park by the roadside and walk across the Slate Quay below the Castle. By road the Town centre is two miles away, and parking can be difficult and expensive.

The Castle was begun by Edward I in 1283, on the site of a Norman motte and bailey, and finished by the first Prince of Wales some 50 years later. It was twice besieged unsuccessfully by Owain Glyndwr, the scene of bitter fighting during the Civil Wars and captured by Parliament forces in 1646, and finally ordered to be demolished in 1660. Much of the interior has vanished, but the outer walls were spared, and are still in remarkably good condition. Some authorities doubt whether Edward II could have been born in the Castle in 1284, when building had only started a year before, but as an infant he was shown to the people of Wales as their Prince from Queen Eleanor's Gate, and finally installed as Prince of Wales in 1301 when he was 17.

The medieval town walls, contemporary with the Castle, are very well preserved but enclose only a small part of the modern town. In Castle Square, just up the slope from the Slate Quay, there is a statue of David Lloyd George, one-time Constable of the Castle, and several buildings with good Georgian frontages. The town has several fine 19th
(Continued on Page 23.)

Llanwnda

The Normanesque Parish Church (1848) is notable mainly for the large and ornate memorials in the churchyard. The prominent chapel with a spire on your right just before Point F is late Victorian.

Diversion to Nantlle and Snowdonia

We strongly recommend you to turn aside in Penygroes into the Nantlle valley, passing on your way the terraced miners' cottages and slate quarries of Talysarn. The road passes Llyn Nantlle and climbs through a mountain pass until you come in sight of the western slopes of Snowdon itself rising from the village of Rhyd-ddu, the starting point of one of the routes to the summit. (See *North Snowdonia by Car* — Map 6, Page 12.) The distance from Penygroes to Rhyd-ddu is about 7½ miles.

1. Caernarfon Castle

2. Monument in Llanwnda Churchyard

3. Chapel at Llanwnda

4. Snowdon from Nantlle — Rhyd-ddu Road

5. Chapel at Penygroes

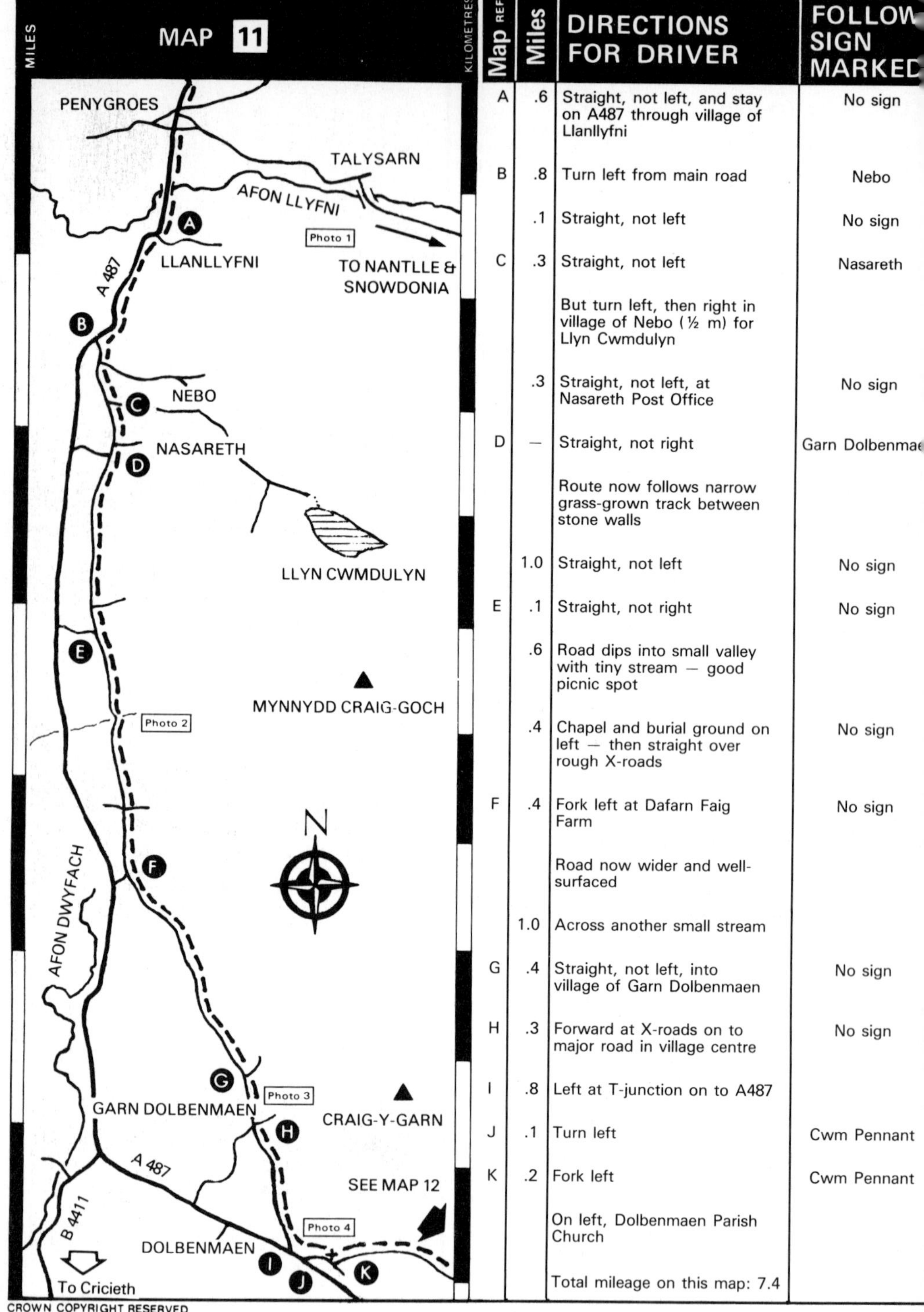

Map REF	Miles	DIRECTIONS FOR DRIVER	FOLLOW SIGN MARKED
A	.6	Straight, not left, and stay on A487 through village of Llanllyfni	No sign
B	.8	Turn left from main road	Nebo
	.1	Straight, not left	No sign
C	.3	Straight, not left	Nasareth
		But turn left, then right in village of Nebo (½ m) for Llyn Cwmdulyn	
	.3	Straight, not left, at Nasareth Post Office	No sign
D	—	Straight, not right	Garn Dolbenmaen
		Route now follows narrow grass-grown track between stone walls	
	1.0	Straight, not left	No sign
E	.1	Straight, not right	No sign
	.6	Road dips into small valley with tiny stream — good picnic spot	
	.4	Chapel and burial ground on left — then straight over rough X-roads	No sign
F	.4	Fork left at Dafarn Faig Farm	No sign
		Road now wider and well-surfaced	
	1.0	Across another small stream	
G	.4	Straight, not left, into village of Garn Dolbenmaen	No sign
H	.3	Forward at X-roads on to major road in village centre	No sign
I	.8	Left at T-junction on to A487	
J	.1	Turn left	Cwm Pennant
K	.2	Fork left	Cwm Pennant
		On left, Dolbenmaen Parish Church	
		Total mileage on this map: 7.4	

Llanllyfni

This is a typical quarrymen's village of slate-roofed terrace houses strung out along the main road. The Victorian church is dedicated to St. Gredfyn; the chapels, particularly Capel Ebenezer and Capel Moriah, are rather more interesting.

Llyn Cwmdulyn

This little reservoir at the end of a rough track beyond the village of Nebo (see Route Directions) nestles at the foot of a sheer rock face — Craig Cwmdulyn. The peak to the east immediately behind the lake is Garnedd Goch, 701 m (2301 ft), and the one to the south is Mynydd Craig Goch, 608 m (1996 ft).

Dolbenmaen and Garn Dolbenmaen

These are quite separate villages — Garn Dolbenmaen is much the larger and stands some way up the hillside away from A487; it has a wide main street with some attractively grouped buildings. Dolbenmaen has been by-passed only recently, and is little more than a hamlet; the tiny church has an 18th century lych-gate.

Caernarfon *(Continued from Page 21.)*

century buildings, notably the County Hall close to the Castle entrance, the covered market in Palace Street, and the Conservative Club in Market Street.

Apart from the walls, little earlier than the 19th century remains, but there are a few 17th and 18th century houses, the 16th century Black Boy Inn in Northgate Street, and the 14th century garrison church of St. Mary built into the north-western corner of the town walls. There is an excellent leaflet written by the pupils of a local school, and published by the Town Council, describing a 'Town Trail' which takes you round old Caernarfon, and contains much fascinating information about the town and its history. The site of the Roman fort of Segontium was half a mile or so inland. It was excavated by Sir Mortimer Wheeler in 1920, and much of the original walls plan is clearly defined. There is an interesting small museum of local discoveries.

GLOSSARY OF SOME WELSH PLACE NAMES
continued from page 13

Foel—a rounded hill	Llefn—smooth
Gaer—a camp	Llithrig—slippery
Gallt—a slope	Llwyd—grey
Garn—an eminence	Llyn—a lake
Glas—blue-green	Llys—a hall
Glyn—a deep valley	Maen—block of stone
Goch—red	Maes—field or meadow
Gors—a swamp	Mawr—large
Groes—a cross	Mign—a bog
Hafod—a summer	Moel—a barren hill
dwelling	Morfa—a flat seashore
Hebog—a hawk	Mur—a wall
Hen—old	Mynydd—a mountain
Isaf—lower	Nant—a brook
Llan—a church	Newydd—new

Continued on page 31

1. *Slate Quarry at Talysarn*

2. *Our Route near Point E*

3. *Garn Dolbenmaen*

4. *Dolbenmaen*

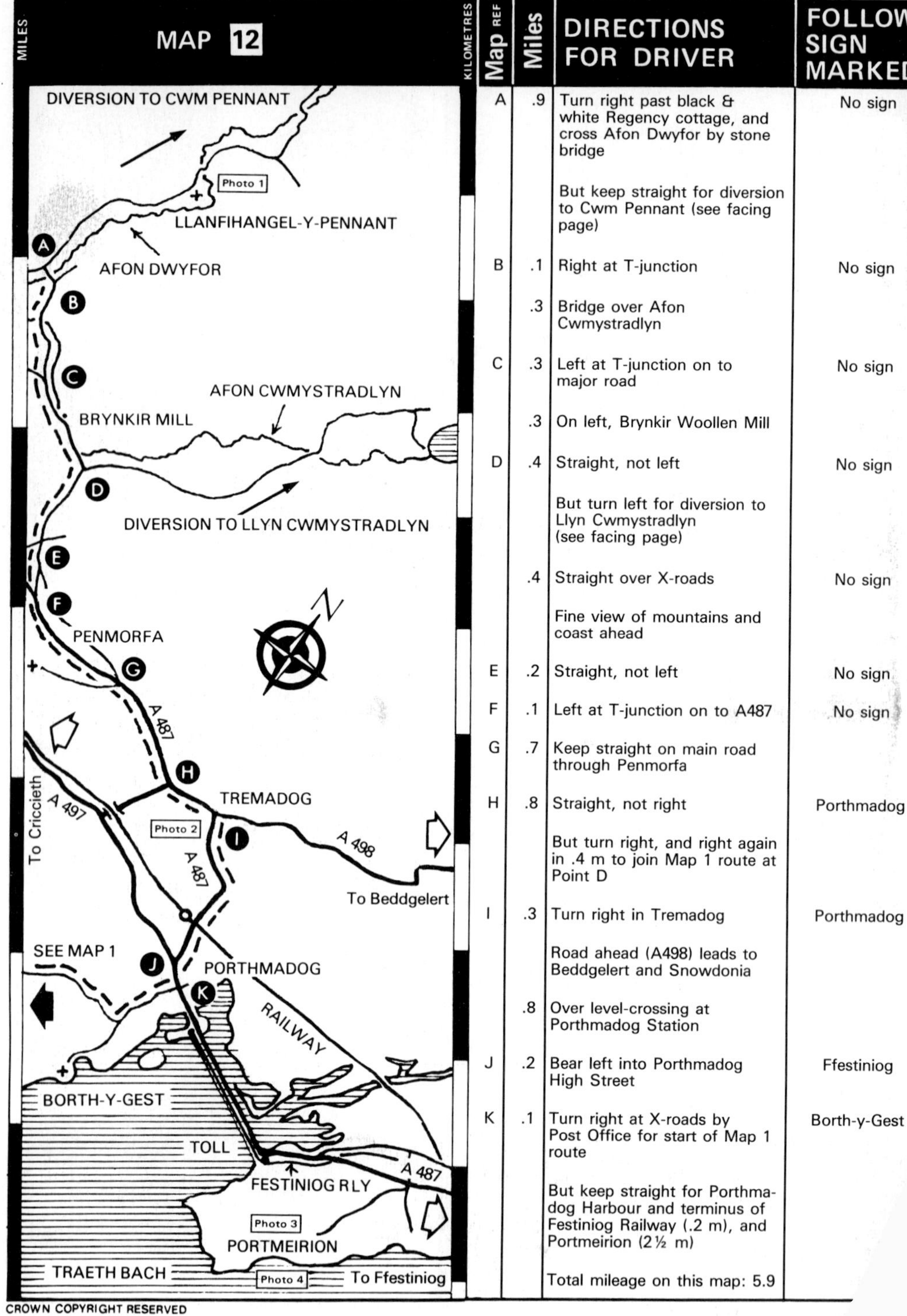

Map REF	Miles	DIRECTIONS FOR DRIVER	FOLLOW SIGN MARKED
A	.9	Turn right past black & white Regency cottage, and cross Afon Dwyfor by stone bridge	No sign
		But keep straight for diversion to Cwm Pennant (see facing page)	
B	.1	Right at T-junction	No sign
	.3	Bridge over Afon Cwmystradlyn	
C	.3	Left at T-junction on to major road	No sign
	.3	On left, Brynkir Woollen Mill	
D	.4	Straight, not left	No sign
		But turn left for diversion to Llyn Cwmystradlyn (see facing page)	
	.4	Straight over X-roads	No sign
		Fine view of mountains and coast ahead	
E	.2	Straight, not left	No sign
F	.1	Left at T-junction on to A487	No sign
G	.7	Keep straight on main road through Penmorfa	
H	.8	Straight, not right	Porthmadog
		But turn right, and right again in .4 m to join Map 1 route at Point D	
I	.3	Turn right in Tremadog	Porthmadog
		Road ahead (A498) leads to Beddgelert and Snowdonia	
	.8	Over level-crossing at Porthmadog Station	
J	.2	Bear left into Porthmadog High Street	Ffestiniog
K	.1	Turn right at X-roads by Post Office for start of Map 1 route	Borth-y-Gest
		But keep straight for Porthmadog Harbour and terminus of Festiniog Railway (.2 m), and Portmeirion (2½ m)	
		Total mileage on this map: 5.9	

Diversion to Cwm Pennant

You can follow the road into Cwm Pennant from Point A for more than four miles, with the Afon Dwyfor always close by, and the western heights of Snowdonia gathering to the north and east. After the first mile you can see the simple Victorian church of Llanfihangel-y-Pennant on the river bank to your right, and soon you cross an ancient stone bridge — Pont Gyfyng — in the shadow of a rocky hill known as Craig Isallt; the scenery here is beautiful.

Brynkir Woollen Mill

Originally powered by the Afon Cwmystradlyn, this mill is still working and open to the public.

Diversion to Llyn Cwmystradlyn

This reservoir in a remote mountain valley is about 2½ miles from the main road. On your way you will pass the gaunt ruin of Ynyspandy slate mill.

Penmorfa

Half a mile down a lane to the south of this village straggling along A487 you will find the old parish church, which has a memorial to Sir John Owen, a Royalist leader in the 17th century, who was condemned to death, but secured a reprieve and lived to see the restoration of Charles II.

Tremadog

This little town was developed by William Madocks, M.P., the founder of Porthmadog, as part of his scheme to make Porth Dinllaen on the north coast of Lleyn the port for a new mail route to Ireland. It was built during the first years of the 19th century on reclaimed land, and the buildings facing the open square have an attractive unity of design — a good example of early town planning. High in the woods to the east of Tremadog is the Regency house of Tan-yr-Allt, built by Madocks and later rented by the poet Shelley. T. E. Lawrence, of World War I desert fame, was born in Tremadog.

Porthmadog

Early in the 19th century, William Madocks, M.P. for Boston in Lincolnshire, gained Parliament's approval to build the mile-long embankment known as the Cob across the mouth of the Glaslyn Estuary. This reclaimed more than 5000 acres from the sea, and made Porthmadog the major port for the growing slate industry. The trading schooners and ketches have long since departed — all except one, the S. V. Garlandstone, now moored to the quayside as the main exhibit of the Maritime Museum. The harbour is now filled with yachts, and pleasant modern flats and houses have been built on the quays. Today Porthmadog is a good centre from which to explore the whole of the Lleyn and Snowdonia (see the companion guides — *North* and *South Snowdonia by Car*). Recommended short day excursions from the town include the Llechwedd Slate Caverns and the Gloddfa Ganol Mountain Centre at Blaenau Ffestiniog, and Portmeirion Italian Village. (See page 29.)

Festiniog Railway (See page 27.)

1. *Llanfihangel-y-Pennant Church*

2. *Tremadog*

3. *Portmeirion Village*

4. *Portmeirion Hotel*

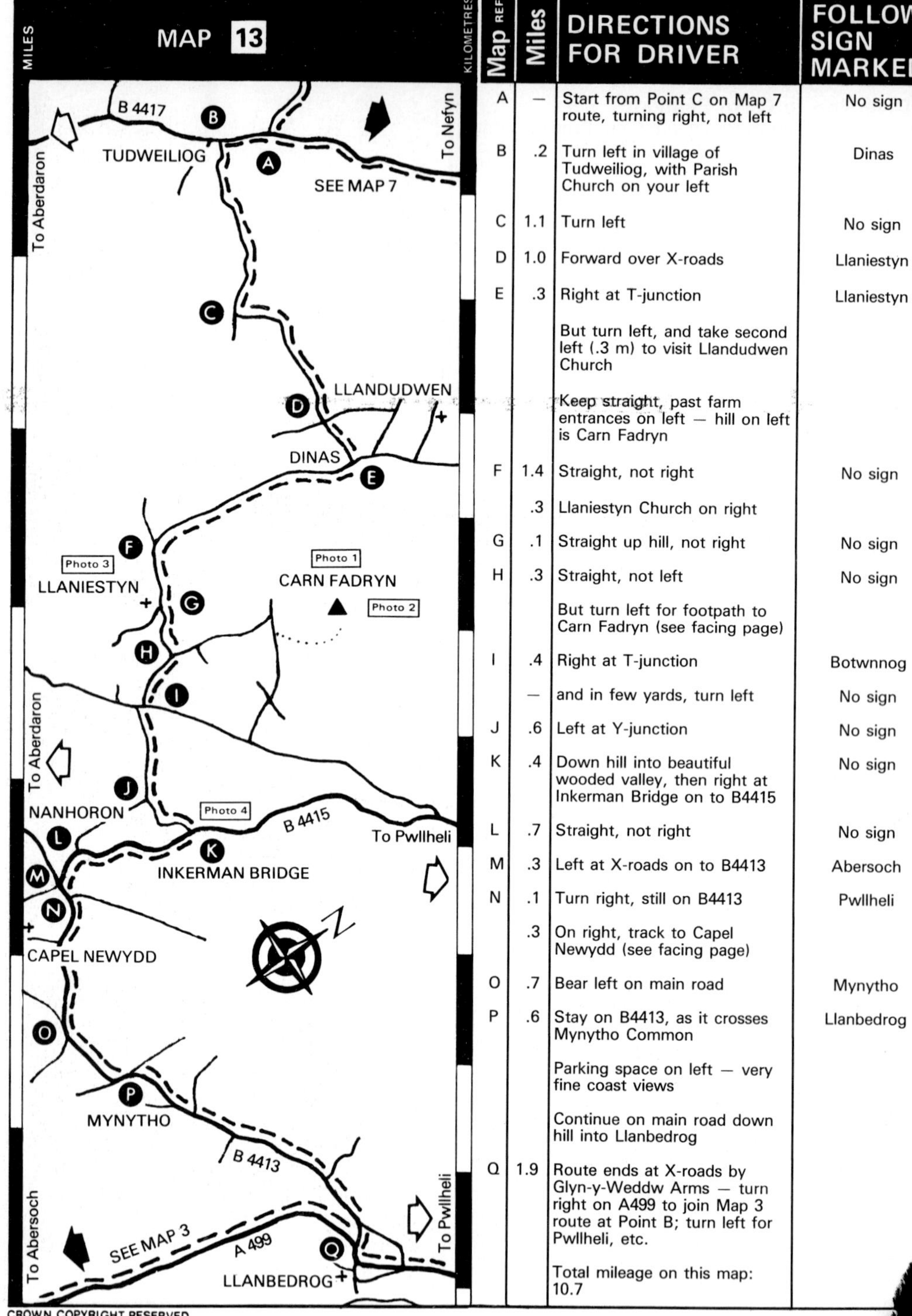

Map REF	Miles	DIRECTIONS FOR DRIVER	FOLLOW SIGN MARKED
A	—	Start from Point C on Map 7 route, turning right, not left	No sign
B	.2	Turn left in village of Tudweiliog, with Parish Church on your left	Dinas
C	1.1	Turn left	No sign
D	1.0	Forward over X-roads	Llaniestyn
E	.3	Right at T-junction	Llaniestyn
		But turn left, and take second left (.3 m) to visit Llandudwen Church	
		Keep straight, past farm entrances on left — hill on left is Carn Fadryn	
F	1.4	Straight, not right	No sign
	.3	Llaniestyn Church on right	
G	.1	Straight up hill, not right	No sign
H	.3	Straight, not left	No sign
		But turn left for footpath to Carn Fadryn (see facing page)	
I	.4	Right at T-junction	Botwnnog
	—	and in few yards, turn left	No sign
J	.6	Left at Y-junction	No sign
K	.4	Down hill into beautiful wooded valley, then right at Inkerman Bridge on to B4415	No sign
L	.7	Straight, not right	No sign
M	.3	Left at X-roads on to B4413	Abersoch
N	.1	Turn right, still on B4413	Pwllheli
	.3	On right, track to Capel Newydd (see facing page)	
O	.7	Bear left on main road	Mynytho
P	.6	Stay on B4413, as it crosses Mynytho Common	Llanbedrog
		Parking space on left — very fine coast views	
		Continue on main road down hill into Llanbedrog	
Q	1.9	Route ends at X-roads by Glyn-y-Weddw Arms — turn right on A499 to join Map 3 route at Point B; turn left for Pwllheli, etc.	
		Total mileage on this map: 10.7	

Tudweiliog

An exposed village on a hill-top, with a pleasant-looking inn, and a dull Victorian church, rebuilt by Sir Gilbert Scott in 1850.

Llandudwen Church

This is a tiny medieval church, beautifully kept and standing alone in open farmland within a close-mown walled enclosure — a visual gem well worth the short detour.

Llaniestyn

In a wooded valley at the foot of Carn Fadryn, this peaceful village has another well-cared-for medieval church, distinguished by an unusual musicians' gallery.

Carn Fadryn

On the summit of this prominent hill, 371 m (1217 ft), there is an important Iron Age hill-fort, and a large flat stone known as 'Arthur's Table'. There is an easy path to the top from the telephone box in the hamlet of Garn (left at Point H, and in .6 mile turn right at T-junction). We were shown the way by a friendly dog from the village shop.

Capel Newydd

A farm track on the right between Point N and O (see Route Directions) leads to the earliest surviving Nonconformist chapel in North Wales, a simple barn-like structure with earth floor and box pews.

Mynytho

This scattered parish occupies much of the high ground inland from Llandbedrog and Abersoch. Most of it is common land, on which there are several springs and ancient wells.

Llandbedrog (See page 7)

Festiniog Railway (See Map 12).

The narrow gauge (1 ft 11½ in) line was built to bring slate from the quarries at Blaenau Ffestiniog to the docks at Porthmadog and for a time also carried passengers. It was closed in 1939, and part of the line was submerged by a new reservoir. Since being reopened by a group of enthusiasts, it has become a popular tourist attraction, with regular services as far as Blaenau Ffestiniog. The scenery throughout the journey is spectacular as the train climbs from sea level and follows the wooded slopes above the Vale of Ffestiniog. The steam engines include some locally-built double-ended locomotives, and there are 1st and 3rd class coaches, buffet cars, and an observation coach — well worth the extra charge.

1. *Carn Fadryn*

2. *View from Carn Fadryn*

3. *Cottages at Llaniestyn*

4. *Springtime near Inkerman Bridge*

MAP 14

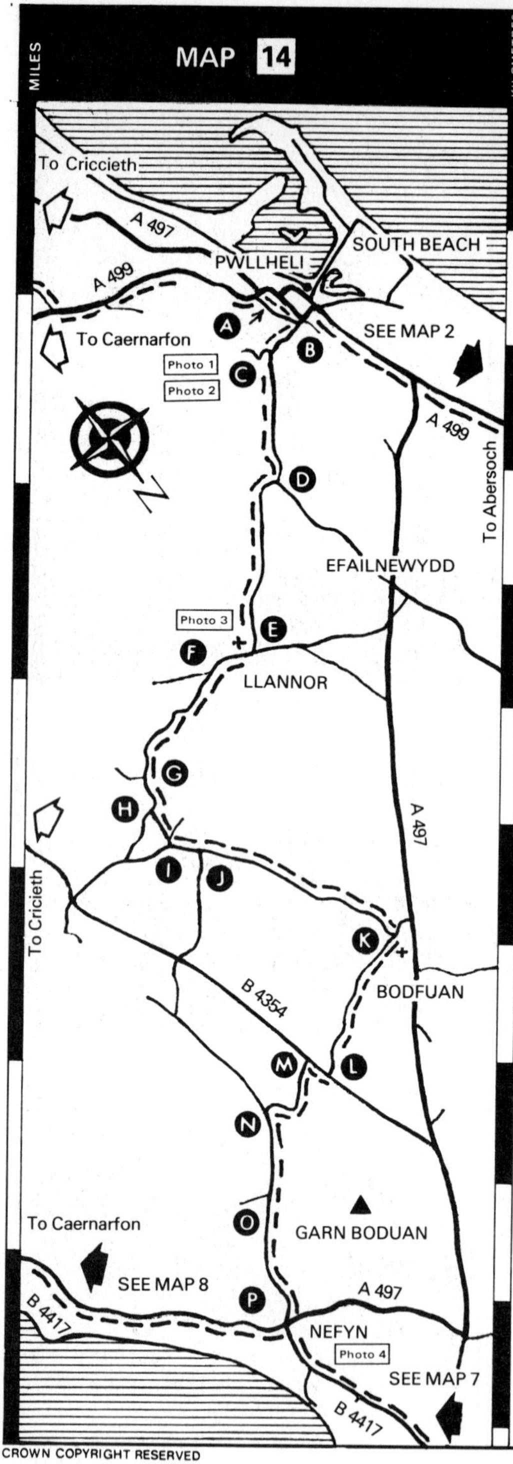

CROWN COPYRIGHT RESERVED

Map REF	Miles	DIRECTIONS FOR DRIVER	FOLLOW SIGN MARKED
A	—	Start along Pwllheli High Street, at the junction with New Street (Point I on Map 2)	
B	.1	Continue forward to end of High Street, and turn right at X-roads into Strood Moch (Gaol St)	Llannor
	.1	Keep up hill to left of Salem Chapel	No sign
C	.3	Bear left on major road	Efailnewydd
D	.7	Fork right at Y-junction	Llannor
E	1.1	Right at T-junction in Llannor	No sign
F	.3	Left at Y-junction	No sign
G	.7	Straight, not right	No sign
H	.2	Turn left	No sign
I	.2	Forward over X-roads	No sign
J	.1	Straight, not right	No sign
K	1.2	Turn sharp right	No sign
		But turn left, then right on to main road to visit Bodfuan Church (.2 m)	
		Route continues past Bodfuan Hall (now hotel) and through dense woodland	
L	.8	Right at T-junction	No sign
M	.1	Turn left	No sign
		Hill on left is Garn Boduan	
N	.4	Left at T-junction	No sign
O	.5	Straight, not right	No sign
		Panoramic view of Nefyn, Morfa Nefyn, and Porth Dinllaen ahead	
P	.7	Bear right into Nefyn, and turn right at X-roads to join Map 7 route at Point I	Llithfaen
		Total mileage on this map: 7.5	

Pwllheli (See page 5)

Llannor

In a rather dull village with some ugly council houses, the church has a bold outline, with stepped gables above a plain tower; there is a late Roman tombstone in the porch.

Bodfuan

The neo-Norman sandstone church (1894) beside the main road has a X-shaped interior and some good monuments of the Wynn family of Bodvean. The Hall, early 18th century with Victorian additions, almost hidden in dense woods of beeches and rhododendrons, is now an hotel. The prominent hill just south of Nefyn is Garn Boduan, 280 m (918 ft), and has remains of an Iron Age fort near its summit. (Bodfuan, Bodvean, and Boduan are all variations of the same name.)

Nefyn (See Map 7)

Although there is little to show for it now, this place has a long history. In 1224 King Edward I of England celebrated his victory over Llewellyn the Last by holding a tournament here, and in 1355 it was designated one of the ten Royal Boroughs of Wales. No buildings remain from that period, and most of the town is comparatively modern. Even the old church of St. Mary, rebuilt in 1820 with a rather narrow tower which has an over-large ship as a weather-vane, is now derelict.

Portmeirion (See Map 12)

Between the estuaries of the rivers Glaslyn and Dwyryd there is a rocky peninsula on which the famous architect, Sir Clough Williams Ellis has created a magnificent 'folly', an Italianate village which has become one of the show-places of North Wales. Set on a densely wooded south facing slope, and surrounded by a wild garden of rhododendrons and azaleas, the village contains an astonishing variety of buildings and architectural fancies, some of which the founder himself rescued from demolition sites elsewhere. Below the village and within a few yards of the sandy shore is the Portmeirion Hotel, converted from an elegant early 19th century house. This has its own 'folly', a trim little concrete sailing ship, 'moored' to the quayside outside the hotel windows. Portmeirion was filmed as the setting for the T.V. series, 'The Prisoner', and was also used for an episode of 'Dr. Who'. It is a place which you must see for yourself, even though the admission charge is deliberately kept high to prevent overcrowding.

1. *Street in Old Pwllheli*

2. *Penlan Fawr Inn, Pwllheli*

3. *Llannor Church*

4. *Three Herrings Inn, Nefyn*

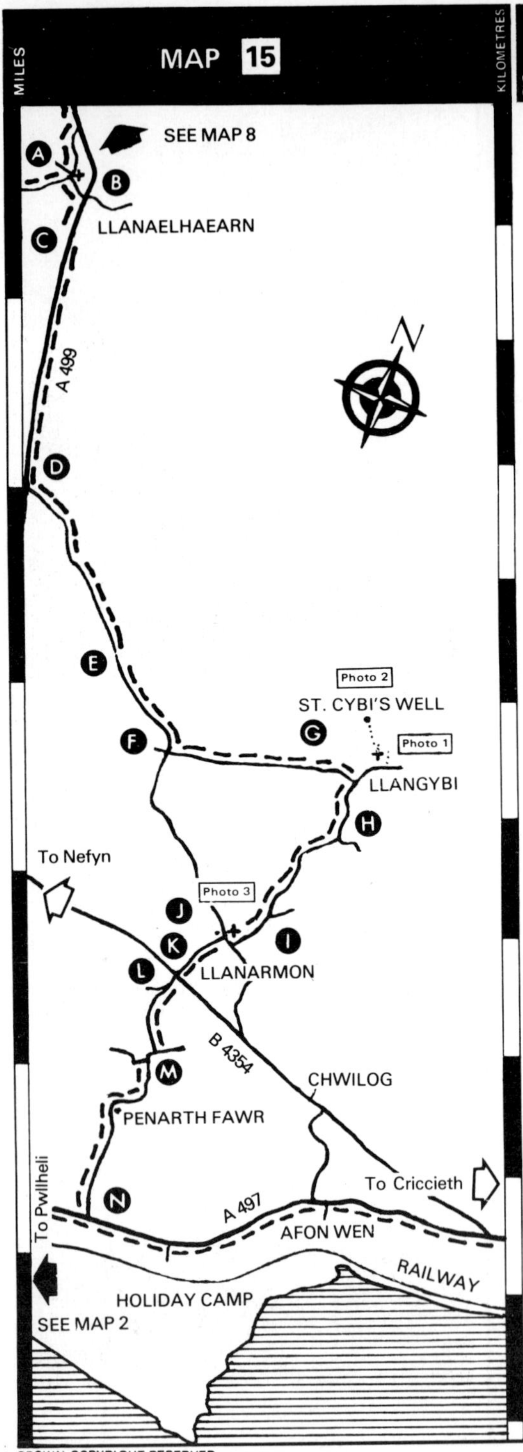

Map REF	Miles	DIRECTIONS FOR DRIVER	FOLLOW SIGN MARKED
A	—	Start in village of Llanaelhaearn, turning right at X-roads (Point C on Map 8 route)	No sign
		Parish Church on left	
B	.1	Right at X-roads on to A499	No sign
C	.2	Straight, not left	No sign
D	1.4	Turn left from A499	Pencaenewydd
E	1.2	Straight over X-roads	Llanarmon
F	.6	Left at X-roads	Llangybi
G	1.0	Right at Y-junction in Llangybi	
		But turn left to visit Llangybi Church and St. Cybi's Well (see facing page)	
H	.4	Turn right	Llanarmon
I	.6	Right at T-junction	No sign
J	.3	Right at T-junction, then fork left, keeping Llanarmon Church and school on your right	Y Ffor
K	.3	Forward at X-roads over B4354	No sign
L	.1	Straight, not right	No sign
M	.4	Right at T-junction	No sign
	.1	Straight, not right	No sign
	.4	Bear left round farm — on left just after corner is Penarth Fawr (medieval hall)	
N	.6	Right at T-junction on to A497 to join Map 2 route at Point D — or turn left for Butlins' Holiday Camp (½ m), Criccieth, Porthmadog, etc.	No sign
		Total mileage on this map: 7.7	

Llanaelhaearn (See also Map 8)

The cruciform Parish Church of this village in the shadow of Yr Eifl dates back to the 12th century, but was very much restored and enlarged at the end of the 19th century. It has a fine 15th or 16th century rood screen and attractive box pews. Several inscribed stones, probably 6th century, were found during restoration, and link the church with the period of the pilgrimages to Bardsey.

Llangybi

A path through the churchyard and over the fields beyond leads to St. Cybi's Well, a roofless stone structure attached to the ruins of a later cottage, which you will find in a valley beneath the wooded slopes of Carn Pentyrch. St. Cybi was a 6th century Cornish saint, and the present simple Parish Church occupies the site of one that he founded. A group of almshouses near the church date from 1760.

Llanarmon

The adjacent church and school were both built in the 15th century; the church has a graceful arcade between its two aisles and a primitive contemporary rood screen.

Penarth Fawr

This well-preserved stone building was the hall of a Welsh gentleman's house of the early 15th century, and contains some fine timber work and an impressive stone fireplace. The roof and windows are however comparatively modern. It is open at all reasonable times, but be careful not to obstruct the roadway or damage the grass verges when parking.

GLOSSARY OF SOME WELSH PLACE NAMES
continued from page 23

Ogof—a cave	Tan—under
Pair—a cauldron	Tomen—a mound
Pen—a peak or top	Traeth—sandy shore
Pentre—a village	Tri—three
Perfedd—centre	Ty—a house
Plas—a mansion	Uchaf—upper or higher
Pont—a bridge	Waun—moorland
Porth—a port	Wen—white
Rhaeadr—a waterfall	Wrach—a witch
Rhyd—a passage or ford	Y, Yr—the
Sarn—a causeway	Yn—in
Sych—dry	
Tal—a brow of a hill, or headland	

1. St. Cybi's Church

2. St. Cybi's Well

3. Llanarmon Church

INDEX